DATE DUE

MAR 2 1 1996	
APR _ 1 1997	

BRODART   Cat. No. 23-221

VICTIM

VICTIM

Caught in the Environmental Web

Bruce G. Siminoff

Glenbridge Publishing Ltd.

Library of Congress Catalog Card Number: LC 92-71366

International Standard Book Number: 0-944435-19-X

Printed in the U. S. A.

To the victims of environmental hysteria.

Contents

Foreword

Protection of our environment is the public policy issue of the second half of the twentieth century that has engendered the broadest popular public support. Conservation of natural resources, prevention of air and water pollution, and remediation of contaminated sites have all been the subject of federal and state legislative enactments. Unfortunately, the expedient enactment of such politically attractive legislation has often been at the expense of practicality, fairness, and justice. For example, in the wake of the discovery of the Love Canal in New York and Valley of the Drums in Kentucky, a vast array of federal and state laws was enacted to deal with the remediation of hazardous substance discharges, both old and new. Recognizing the sheer number of sites to be addressed, our state and federal legislators designed legislation that satisfied the political demands to deal with these issues and, at the same time, avoided criticism concerning the cost of these programs by shifting virtually all costs to the private sector.

While the concept that "the polluter pays" is one which is intuitively attractive, these statutes incorporated three very severe liability principles: strict liability, joint and several liability, and retroactive liability. As a result of strict liability, disposal activities which were legal in the 1950s and 1960s, and in compliance with permits in the 1970s, became the basis for liability in the 1980s. In other words, responsibility for remediation could be imposed without any showing of culpability.

Under the principle of joint and several liability, entities that contributed a mere fraction of a percent of the allegedly offensive material at a site could be held responsible by the government for the remediation of the entire site. In some, but not all legislation, a bone was thrown to the regulated community allowing it to seek contribution from other responsible parties, but only after the target "deep pocket" had spent considerable funds. Finally, liability was deemed to be retroactive, thus rendering activities undertaken years or even decades ago the subject of liability. Each one of these three principles of liability has severe consequences; when combined they have resulted in a draconian liability scheme.

Bruce Siminoff recounts a number of situations in which parties without culpability have been held responsible, often to the point of bankruptcy, for the remediation of conditions they did not create.

The environmental legislative enactments of the past several decades have also consistently delegated significant powers to administrative agencies. Our civil servants not only administer environmental programs, but literally design them. The enabling legislation frequently has provided only the most general guidelines allowing free reign to the regulators to enact regulations that have the power of law. Many of these enactments, however, involve basic public policy decisions that ought to be made by our legislators. For example, in selecting the appropriate degree of risk used to determine clean-up levels, agencies have grasped at the most conservative risk factors, such as a one-in-a-million increase in lifetime cancer risk. This choice of a risk standard is based on a very thin reed—a single legislative enactment that adopted this risk factor as an appropriate standard for drinking water. The regulators have chosen to utilize this standard along with a series of very conservative scientific assumptions to create an exceedingly stringent remedial model. While no one would rationally argue for increased risk to society, extremely conservative marginal standards fail to recognize the inherent risks we face each day when we drive to work, fly on an airplane, have our clothes dry cleaned, or drink diet soft drinks. Nevertheless, our legislators have abdicated their responsibility to choose reasonable standards and have allowed regulators to define standards that cost industry literally billions of dollars. Clearly, effective legislative oversight of the administration of regulatory programs is wanting.

A further manipulation of the "polluter pays" principle is that many environmental programs have become entirely fee- and penalty-based. Many programs have thus been distracted from the purported goal of environmental protection. These programs now focus on the generation of permits and paperwork. Substantial fees are charged for the issuance of permits and penalties imposed for their violation. These fees and penalties have been plowed back into the programs to support further staff employment. Our federal and state administrative codes are filled with fee-supported regulatory programs which impose no substantive standards and achieve no environmental good, but generate a tremendous amount of work for government agencies and impose a tremendous financial and regulatory burden on the regulated community. All of this occurs without any concomitant environmental benefit.

The author has exposed significant flaws in the crazy-quilt array of environmental statutes and regulations. He demonstrates the unintended side effects of these programs—an anti-urban, anti-manufacturing public policy that enriches the service industry, saps the strength of our economy, tramples our constitutional rights, and accomplishes little by way of environmental protection and improvement. He has not only exposed the essence of this inequitable system, but offers a refreshing free market solution.

Edward A. Hogan, Esq.,
Chair, Environmental Department,
Prozio, Bromberg & Newman, P.C.,
Morristown, New Jersey
and New York City

Preface

This book is not a debate about whether our environment should be protected. We must live in a clean environment. It is about the threats to constitutional standards of due process and to traditional American notions of fair play posed by the present approaches to environmental clean-up under both New Jersey and federal laws.

Is a $25,000 fine for throwing a bottle into the ocean just or unjust? In New Jersey the movement of rocks in a stream or river without an environmental impact statement can be a crime. If a company or business runs out of money and leaves hazardous substances on their premises for several months— the next owners could face criminal charges.

The words found in the New Jersey Environmental Clean-Up Responsibility Act (ECRA) regulations "jointly and severally, without regard to fault," are not representative of a just or free people. When a government acquires powers that threaten personal liberty, then we have begun to reverse over seven hundred years of individual rights that began with the

Magna Charta in 1215 A.D. There is no place in a free society for any rule or regulation that bears the words "without regard to fault."

The power acquired by the New Jersey Department of Environmental Protection and Energy (N.J.D.E.P.E.) has exceeded that of any police organization in the history of the United States. The NJDEPE

(a) interprets the law (without oversight);
(b) writes the regulations;
(c) assigns the case workers;
(d) issues the orders on a case-by-case basis (without published standards);
(e) levies, collects and retains substantial fees for receipt of paperwork;
(f) assigns enormous paperwork responsibilities to the filer;
(g) assesses fines for noncompliance at astronomical levels and retains the collected proceeds;
(h) retains the appellate process within its organization. If the NJDEPE loses a dispute on an issue, it can and has turned over names to its sister departments (toxic waste, sound control, etc.) that can usually find some area of noncompliance. If one takes a case to court and wins, that person must still obtain normal operating permits from NJDEPE sister departments, sometimes difficult after beating them in court. In short, tyranny of the environment reigns in New Jersey, as well as many other parts of America.

In the last decade we have ceded, without a fight, many hitherto treasured rights to the siren song of the environment. Some of these invaded areas encompass: private property, due process, search and seizure, and ex post facto legislation.

This book will show what happens when a democratic government permits an agency to exceed its bounds and assumes sweeping powers for itself. It shows how comfortable business and citizens in America have become; as long as we have our luxuries, we no longer care about the loss of our individual freedoms. Many say "it will never happen to me."

Many executives feel "it's a business expense;" it's a bad regulation but "we will leave a few employees here and move the rest out." "We can make the product overseas," are all common laments. Fighting a bad rule or law is left to a few protesters. Only a few will take the time and energy to speak up forcefully or fight errant government agencies. Business remains silent, afraid to run afoul of the regulators.

But citizens must find their bravery somewhere and stand up to despotic behavior. Our rights are being threatened by "Environmental Extremism." "ECRA" is a thinking process as well as a law. ECRA is now used as a substitute word for environmental extremism, of which it has become a national synonym.

There is no reason to believe that freedom, justice, and due process must be extinguished, simply because we wish to breathe fresh air.

Acknowledgments

The author wishes to thank the following individuals for assistance in the preparation of this book: Edward A. Hogan, Esq., Mark K. Lipton, Esq. and James A. Keene, for editing; JoAnn Chaplin for typing; Joseph Douglass, Ed Croot, Art Biancone, Richard Duprey, and Franklin Reick, for contributions.

For editing and proofreading thanks go to members of my family, Anne E., John A. and James W. Siminoff.

Many quotations were assembled from newspapers and magazines. My appreciation is extended for this material to: *The Star Ledger;* the *New York Times; Wall Street Journal; Investors Business Daily; Forbes* magazine; *Farm Journal; N.J. Success Magazine; Daily Record; The Record; Printing Management Magazine;* the *Easton Express,* the *Observer-Tribune,* and *Business Week.*

I

An Environmental Agency Investigation

It is fitting that during World War II an establishment called United Wallpaper Company ("United"), located in the scenic, hilly Fairmount section of Washington Township, New Jersey, opened for business. However, home decorating was not really the company's marketing plan during World War II, and wallpaper was not a part of its 1942 product line.

It was reported that the company was actually a contractor for the U.S. Army, Chemical Warfare Department. Retired employees said that from 1942 to 1945, United made war munitions. But to the outside world it appeared to be a wallpaper manufacturing company.

All of the former workers agree that they were making napalm bombs. They don't know the exact chemical contents but they do know they inserted jellied gasoline, and some type of gunpowder into the bombs. Napalm is fuel thickened with napthenic acid, coconut oil, oleic acid, and aluminum soap.[1]

Munitions manufacturing during the 1940s was quite different than the 1990s. The environmental responsibilities enforced today upon business and military installations were nonexistent. New Jersey's ECRA (Environmental Clean-Up Responsibility Act) was enacted in 1983. This law placed rigid clean-up responsibilities on business, while various NJDEPE (New Jersey Department of Environmental Protection and Energy) regulations (clean water, clean air, etc.) were designed to enforce stringent operating procedures. Today, there are a myriad of federal EPA requirements also. But rules and regulations of this nature did not exist during World War II, and environmental responsibility was not well understood.

New Jersey companies began their famed iron foundries in the early 1700s, and until recent times, environmental responsibility played a minor role in American business planning. Unfortunately, United Wallpaper evidently followed the same environmentally unsound practices as did many other war contractors during World War II and prior periods.

During the past decade the level of awareness of environmental problems has increased tremendously throughout the military and business community, resulting in forward strides in environmental management by most United States companies.

Unfortunately, this level of awareness and "the current due diligence process did not exist at the beginning of the 1980s, and many property owners, businessmen, and New Jersey citizens fell into a serious 'catch-22' as a result."[2]

It has been reported that leakers, spilled bomb contents, and excess materials were buried behind United's factory during the World War II years. The facility, now known as Cleaveland Industrial Park, may very well have been polluted by our country's war efforts.

> A supervisor in the "powder room" where workers loaded a gunpowder mix in a hole in a side of the bomb stated, "they buried the leakers back in the field. They would take them out at night. They burned some of them off. What they didn't burn, they buried," he said.[3]

Roll the clock forward nearly a half century. New owners purchased control of Cleaveland Industrial Park in 1980. These owners may have been totally unaware of the munition manufacturing activities of United as well as the extent of the pollution that occurred there. In 1980 only former employees were aware of the true story behind the wallpaper company that actually manufactured napalm and incendiary devices.

In addition, because of a lack of sewers in the area, later tenants in the industrial park were required to utilize septic systems that were connected to drainage fields feeding directly into the surrounding ground area, not into a sewer system.

Six years later, in 1986, groundwater pollution on the Morris-Hunterdon County border was, allegedly, traced to this location, and the NJDEPE "redlined" 172 residential water wells on the Washington Township side, as well as 92 water wells on the Tewksbury Township line. In addition, a ban was placed on new well drilling in the area. In 1986 the pollution was evident, but who was responsible and when did it occur? Was it United? Was it other tenants? Was Cleaveland Industrial Park the contamination source?

While officials at the NJDEPE questioned the existence of a polluting munitions facility operating as United Wallpaper, the following letter leaves little doubt as to the type of factory located there:

> I was co-editor of the *Mendham-Chester Tribune,* (during World War II), the predecessor of the *Observer Tribune.* . . . I was surprised that no one told you that the "United Wallpaper" plant at Fairmount made all of the bombs that were dropped on Tokyo in 1945. These incendiary bombs killed more Japanese and destroyed more property and manufacturing capability than the atomic bomb dropped on Nagasaki and Hiroshima.[4]

Two things are critical to an understanding of what ensued after the current purchasers acquired the Cleaveland property. First, ECRA had not been yet enacted, and buyers of real property had no reason to believe that they were assuming liability for the havoc done by others, and second, the surrounding area is visually beautiful. There were no visual signs of contamination that would, in any event, have alerted the purchaser to the problems that lay below the earth's surface.

Under NJDEPE groundwater pollution regulations as well as ECRA rules, it is not necessarily the *polluter* who bears the embarrassment, trauma, financial, and legal responsibility for pollution. *It is the current owner* who initially bears these burdens. That the pollution is forty, one hundred, or two hundred years old, is immaterial. The present owner can be held responsible (civilly and criminally), even though he had no apparent knowledge, caused no harm (and), even if he had launched clean-up efforts of his own. The NJDEPE serves as the prosecutor, court, jury, and assessor/collector of fines. As Governor Kean of New Jersey said:

> The enforcement of ECRA does constitute a process for uncovering the environmental impact of over 100 years of industrial activity in this state, activity that often resulted in environmental contamination. The clean-up of this contamination has become an increased public burden that should be borne by *responsible parties* whenever possible. Please also note that *although ECRA does require the current owner* or operator to clean up the site, this does not preclude that party from pursuing legal actions for cost recovery through the courts.[5]

A major problem with Governor Kean's assertions and the NJDEPE regulations is the definition of the simple words "responsible parties." Why is the current owner the "responsible party?" Under current regulations, a person's entire wealth, business, or estate can be lost to meet clean-up costs and litigation expenses simply because he is the current owner. In New Jersey the victim of pollution can be treated as if *he* is the polluter. And that is what may have occurred in the Cleaveland case:

> In June 1989, the NJDEPE named Eversden L. Clark, the managing partner for the Cleaveland Industrial Center, as the party responsible (PRP) for the polluted water. Cleaveland's attorney, Henry Larner of Short Hills, said he disagrees with the NJDEPE—he believes the pollution dates back to previous owners or tenants of the industrial park and not his client.[6]

But under New Jersey law the *guilty party* is not necessarily the wrongdoer or the person who is identified as the Principal Responsible Party. *Under NJDEPE regulations the Principal Responsible Party is the person or company that currently owns, occupies, or rents the named property.* This enforcement technique is commonly called the "deep pockets approach," since it is usually impossible to find defunct companies, deceased individuals, and the principals of closed bomb factories. It is easier to move against the person standing there, i.e., the current owner. It's also hard to sue the United States Army. But, *easy isn't necessarily just.* Many New Jerseyans, who still favor a constitutional form of government, believe this "deep pockets approach" (attacking the victim of pollution) to be totally wanton and destructive of individual rights.

Whether the final outcome in the Cleaveland case proves the pollution came from the old bomb factory, other tenants, or poor septic management, the people who purchased the industrial park in 1980 may not have been responsible for the pollution of the area ground water. This may have occurred without their knowledge, or prior to their ownership.

Why is it necessary to fine or name an individual as the publicly ridiculed party before you are absolutely sure? Because that's the way it is done under New Jersey and some federal environmental regulations! Until the actual *polluter* is found, why do lives of people have to be disrupted because of the bureaucratic need to name a PRP? People are supposed to be presumed innocent until proven guilty.

Following their own regulations that the current owner is responsible for pollution regardless of when it occurred, the NJDEPE ordered the present owners of Cleaveland to pay

$3,500,000 in fines. When they didn't or couldn't comply, the agency warned that it would enforce the levy through court action:

> The state would sue for three times the cost of the clean-up project, which could be more than $10,000,000, and an uncalculated amount for removal [of the contamination] and containment, according to Dennis Hart, Chief of the DEPE's Bureau of Case Management.[7]

The threat significantly frightened the current owners. In essence, without a trial or being proven guilty of a crime, the present owners could have their property and personal assets threatened by the agency. The alternative, that people in this position could be financially able to sue the United States Army to obtain justice, is impractical as well as absurd!

As the owners were frightened by the state's juggernaut, a tenant, Fabritek Corporation, went out of business. In March and April of 1991 environmental authorities began a clean-up of 200-300 containers of stored solvents and resins, left at the site of the Fabritek Corporation, since neither the owners nor landlords were available. It seems safe to speculate that the owners may have been scared away. While the drums had been left at the location, they were not polluting the environment. According to Richard Cahill, an environmental official, "the containers did not appear to be leaking."[8]

Upon completion of the Fabritek clean-up, which was finished in November 1991, the NJDEPE concluded that that company was not responsible for the aquifer pollution that had occurred at Cleaveland. It was suspected (although not yet proven) that the World War II munitions plant could well have been the culprit.

However, officials of the NJDEPE were still making strange statements about the case.

> We were able to recycle some of the material and that cut down on our costs, said Paul Kahn, the EPA's site manager, explaining he expected the mitigation to cost more than it did. Most of the stuff was neatly labeled, and that cut down on our man-hours, so that cut down on our costs.
>
> Money from the agency's superfund for toxic waste clean-up paid for the mitigation and officials said they will not likely receive compensation from the firm's [Fabritek] owner, John Logan, who now resides in Belgium. He shut down the operation in the late 1980s, officials said.
>
> "It's not an extraditable offense, if you can believe that," Kahn said, noting Logan was in New York recently and met with EPA officials, but said he would not pay for mitigation. "We could sue him in absentia, but he has no assets here in the United States . . ." the State NJDEPE spokesperson, Melissa M. Jaeger, had been quoted as saying that the "owner of the industrial park is considered a potentially responsible party . . . and will be liable for paying for the project."[9]

First, the presumably innocent current owners were fined 3.5 million dollars for water pollution that they probably did not cause, and second, they were expected to be responsible for the abandoned drums of a defunct tenant. How could this injustice happen in America?

Under New Jersey DEPE and some federal regulations (such as superfund) one can be found guilty of pollution and named the PRP by use of the most frightening words ever written by any legislator or bureaucrat: JOINTLY and SEVERALLY, *without regard to fault.*

As the Cleaveland owners found out, you don't have to commit the crime of pollution, you just have to "be there." These words have made landlords responsible for their tenants, banks responsible for borrowers, purchasers responsible for unseen pollution of one hundred years ago, and so on. This perversion of the spirit of traditional American justice has even made people whose property is illegally abused by "midnight dumpers," responsible for the ensuing clean-up. They are, in essence, "jointly and severally liable" since the pollution is on their property. If the *dumped upon party* doesn't clean it up, the victim can be fined or can even wind up in jail.

The above shows graphically how today's approach to environmental clean-up, whether through ECRA, or other sister NJDEPE regulations, work in practice, in real life. Unfortunately, the federal government is not far behind. In New Jersey a PRP is the guilty party by mere ownership of a business or a property. If you are unfortunate enough to be named the PRP, you are *publicly* presumed guilty, an approach opposite to our entire system of justice. In our criminal court system, a murderer is presumed innocent until proven guilty. In New Jersey, under its pollution laws, you must prove that you are "not guilty." In addition, according to Governor Kean's letter, you are given the burden to find and/or sue the guilty party, if locatable. The assertion is that you are guilty because of property ownership—not guilty because of the pollution itself. If you are a lender, bank, or mortgage holder, you can also incur these same liabilities upon foreclosure—since *you then will become the new owner of the property!* In New Jersey, and under some federal regulations, a lender can be named a guilty party by his simple foreclosure of contractually liened premises. Unfortunately, federal regulations do not offer relief, and excessive zeal can produce unfortunate results in a free society.

An item appearing in *Forbes* magazine relates another example of these unfortunate results:

> Who is the most notorious environmental criminal in the United States? Would you believe a Hungarian immigrant named John Pozsgai? Pozsgai, who owns a small truck repair shop was convicted in late 1988 of violating the Clean Water Act. His sentence: three years in the slammer and a $202,000 fine, the stiffest penalty ever for an environmental violation. His crime? Filling in 5 acres of a 14-acre parcel he owns in Morrisville, Pa., (near Trenton, NJ) without a permit.[10]

Mr. Pozsgai would have been better off committing a felony against a person. Most first offense felons get probation.

Nothing shows the frustration of a well-meaning individual better than the case of the C & M Manufacturing Company, a small New Jersey company caught in the jaws of ECRA.

The company owned a one acre piece of industrial property in Nutley, New Jersey, including a 17,400 square foot building. The property was purchased on December 31, 1973, with the intent of eventually becoming a manufacturing facility for the company. Subsequent events precluded this from occurring, and the property was leased from that date until August of 1988 when the tenant closed the doors of his business. At that time, the company sold the property to a firm that was to have taken possession on October 1, 1988. It all sounds easy so far, but it wasn't to be that simple.

The change in ownership of the building triggered ECRA. There was alleged to be a possible contamination problem at the site caused by the former tenants and owners. The current owner cooperated with the state environmental protection agency and did everything possible to rectify the situation.

The owner's experience with ECRA, however, was most frustrating. The paperwork was nightmarish, the rules and regulations could only be interpreted by the most astute attorneys, and the costs of dealing with it could only be borne by substantial companies.

The cost to file the initial papers (found in Appendix III) was $750.00 (state filing fee), plus $6,000 in attorneys fees. The submission report totaled 145 pages. Another report, the Air Quality Report, was only two pages long, but cost $1,000 just for filing fees. According to the owner, "the worst part was that not a dime of this $7,750 paid went toward cleaning up the environment—the stated purpose of ECRA review."[11]

In June of 1989, an inspection of the property by ECRA revealed twelve possible problem areas. The company then had to obtain the services of an environmental consulting firm who would write a report stating that it could remedy these twelve areas. The environmental firm charged $3,000 just to fill out the myriad of forms required, and the NJDEPE (ECRA) charged a $4,500 fee to receive and file the report. That's an additional $7,500—but, once again, no clean-up work had been initiated.

Though the property was to have been occupied in October 1988, because of the ECRA review the new owner had not been allowed to take possession of the property, and it remained vacant. The old owner, however, was required to pay insurance, taxes, and other expenses with no income to offset this expense during the process.

Twenty-eight thousand three hundred dollars had been spent with the environmental consulting firm, $4,800 for tank testing, $27,000 in attorney fees for form preparation, and $26,000 in taxes and insurance since the ECRA review had begun. That's a total of $86,100, plus the ECRA filing fees. The environmental consulting firm estimated that an additional $115,000 would be required to complete the clean-up. The owner had been informed that even if they worked expeditiously, it could take at least another year before the receipt of final ECRA approval.

The owner reported, "being a small business, we have run out of funds to continue to clean up, and no bank will lend us money as long as we are under ECRA review [a real catch-22]." A bank lending money on this project could themselves have become secondarily liable for the clean-up if the owner failed to complete it. This could occur if a bank foreclosed on the property and therefore became the new owner. Hence, no lender would advance funds on an ECRA subject business situation and/or loan.[12]

The owner further stated: "as a result, we had planned to put the clean-up on hold, while lawsuits [were] initiated against former owners and tenants of the property whose work actually caused the environmental damage detected by ECRA. My company has never occupied the property, thus we did not cause any of the damage. These suits could probably take years to reach the courts, but if judgment [would be] in the company's favor, we [would have been] able to recover some of our costs, and [would have been able to] proceed with the environmental clean-up at that time." While this legal action sounds fair and reasonable, the owners were advised by their attorneys that this would not be a viable course of action since putting the clean-up on hold would invite prosecution and fines by the NJDEPE under ECRA.

C & M was a small company caught in the jaws of a law that works exactly in reverse of its intention. The best environmental intentions have paved the ECRA road with such difficulties, unfairness, costs, and delays that only the wealthiest companies could comply.

The broad unfairness of current day environmental hysteria can be more practically understood when reviewing the case of Pappys Diner, located on Union Boulevard in Totowa, New Jersey. The owner, John Tsigounis, had operated that eatery for nearly thirty years, without polluting.

In 1981, in order to expand the parking lot for his patrons, he purchased property adjacent to his diner. The purchase price totalled $200,000. Unfortunately for the owner, the property was a former Sunoco gas station. Not long afterwards, NJDEPE officials told Tsigounis that the gas station had been polluted by leaking hydrocarbons stored in the underground tanks. He was given 120 days to launch and finish a clean-up. Said Tsigounis:

> Clean-up costs could run into the millions, putting the business and everything worked for over the last thirty years at risk. Failure to meet that deadline could result in fines of $50,000 per day. It's a real tragedy. I am going to lose everything I own. They are going to take everything I worked for.[13]

That Tsigounis was the innocent victim of pollution that he did not cause, won no sympathy from the NJDEPE enforcers. John Trela, Assistant Commissioner for Hazardous Waste, NJDEPE, said, "If you don't do it (clean-up) we'll seek treble damages. If the clean-up costs $10 million, we'll seek $30 million. It is a tremendous financial incentive [to force innocents to comply]."[14]

There is no question that skewering an innocent party with treble damages is a great incentive. But for whom? The approach sounds like Tsarist Russia. In the British-American tradition this form of government terrorism was ended when King John was forced to sign the Magna Charta on June 15, 1215 A.D. The Magna Charta represented a statement of principles that established personal protections and guarantees in regulations or legislative acts. It was a forerunner of our Constitution with its "due process" concept 574 years later. Unfortunately, the concept of due process seems not to exist with the NJDEPE or in the perceived mission of some environmental extremists.

John Tsigounis stated that he spent nearly $40,000 for legal and consulting fees, testing, etc. But due to "joint and several liability, without regard to fault," no bank would lend funds to him for this project. He has repeatedly contacted Sunoco, the former owner, but to no avail. "We're up against a billion dollar giant; I'm holding the bag. I don't think this is justice," said Tsigounis.[15]

Being fined, held up to ridicule, and having your business or assets destroyed unfairly is a deplorable action. Facing criminal sanctions and/or prison is quite another thing. On February 17, 1991, *The Star Ledger* reported:

> A state grand jury in Trenton indicted the president of a former Irvington, New Jersey, precious metals business on charges of abandoning toxic pollutants or hazardous wastes and related environmental crimes, the state Attorney General's Office said.
>
> The indictment charges Hargovind Govani, 53, of Livingston with abandoning his business at 514 Lyons Avenue and leaving hazardous and toxic wastes inside the structure.

Govani also was charged with unlawful disposal of hazardous waste and creating widespread injury or damage, officials said.

Govani was shocked by the indictment, but expects to be able to prove his innocence.

"As far as I'm concerned, I haven't done anything wrong," he said.

Govani said he was forced to close his company, Silsonix, in March 1989 due to mounting financial losses. After shutting down, he said an additional nine months was spent cleaning the 80,000 square foot, three story structure. Govani said he never abandoned the building but was trying to obtain financial backing to reopen. By the end of 1989, his money ran out, he said.

I have $3 million worth of equipment in the building. Why would I abandon it? I was doing whatever I could to keep my business going.[16]

It is critical to note that sealed and nonleaking drums of oil, solvents, paints and thinners are considered toxic or hazardous wastes. By the simple act of definition a person or company can therefore be accused of storing hazardous wastes. Any substances can be included by the mere trick of promulgating a pertinent regulation. For example, in New Jersey, oil is a hazardous waste, and in California this definition is extended to caffeine (coffee). Under various regulations, typewriter correction fluid, acetic acid (vinegar), and nail polish remover all bear this label. Under similar regulations First Aid Squads have been told to clearly label Saline Solution (H_2O + NACL, i.e, Salt Water).

In the Govani case it is believed that oil, paint, and solvents were the culprits. The real trap is the power given to agencies to write wide and overbearing regulations, which can snare anyone unlucky enough to be in their way.

The extension of environmental overzealousness to make criminal examples of businessmen was bound to occur. It was only a matter of time. But this businessman's crime may just have been "running out of money." In New Jersey if you don't have the cash to complete a clean-up, you can be fined, lose your assets, and perhaps your liberty. No bank will loan you the funds, because they can become secondarily liable for the clean-up. And you cannot store hazardous wastes (including plain old motor oil) indefinitely on your premises, since it runs afoul of other related waste regulations. These rules have time-period parameters, such as sixty or ninety days for such storage. In New Jersey oil is considered a hazardous waste. It is the only state to do so.

By making oil a hazardous waste, every clean-up can become excessively complicated. If oil were treated simply as a "waste material," as in most other states, clean-ups would be simpler and less costly.

Consider the massive power that a state agency has acquired by enforcing environmental regulations in this punitive manner. In New Jersey you can be publicly named the PRP even though innocent, be fined even though not the polluter, have your assets and property threatened, and be placed in a three year paperwork nightmare. Your crime— "ownership." Your protection is to appeal to the courts. But, it's a Hobson's choice; you can be made penniless whether you win or lose. Constitutional protections become seriously compromised under this enforcement methodology, such as (1) due process; (2) innocence until proven guilty; (3) right of private property; (4) habeas corpus, and (5) ex post facto legislation.

There is no question that pollution is reprehensible. But it is truly unfortunate that, contrary to our historical legal process, innocent people must be assumed to be guilty. In the long term, an enforcement mentality of this type will destroy credibility, manufacturing jobs, the tax base, the business climate, and the valued liberty of citizens.

There is an alternative approach. A cooperative effort could be launched by the environmental protectors, legislature, business, labor, and citizens' groups. This approach would work better and faster, because it would encourage a total unified commitment. Current law and regulations make it impossible for a united approach, since the induced atmosphere is one of fear and intimidation. This destroys all chance of real cooperation.

Environmental hysteria takes strange forms with sometimes unbelievable results. The following story appeared in the Chester, New Jersey, *Observer Tribune* on March 9, 1989:

> CHESTER TWP., N.J. Leaves may tumble down but they had best not roll into the lake. Cynthia Strelec of Selma Boulevard learned the hard way.
>
> On October 25, she received a summons for "placing debris in and or adjacent to a waterway."
>
> Strelec attended Monday's Township Council meeting to ask the council what she could do about the summons she received from the State Police for "polluting the river."
>
> As Strelec told the story, she raked the leaves from her yard and dumped them, along with some brush, over the fence at the rear of her property.
>
> The leaves came to rest on the embankment of Lake Lillian, which is in the Black River Wildlife Management Area. Strelec said that she and other neighbors had done the same thing every year since moving to the township 14 years ago. The fence is about 15 feet away from the water.

The results this time were different.

On Wednesday, October 25, she says that she noticed a man walking along the embankment behind her property. A short time later, she saw two men in a boat, apparently taking pictures. At about 10:15 a.m. she said that she was approached by the men, who identified themselves as State Policemen.

After determining she was the homeowner, an officer issued her a summons. She learned later by letter the offense carried a $100 fine and court costs of $15.

Strelec said that a neighbor had received a similar summons and had paid the fine.

Strelec said that she was unaware that she was violating a law.

"I was not dumping them into the water. They were on the embankment," she said in a phone interview Tuesday.

The Strelecs want the township to have a leaf collection program but there are no plans to institute such a program.

"I don't know what to do with the leaves," she said. "I'm leaving them in a huge pile in the backyard."

Township Attorney, Barry Markowitz, expressed his sympathy but said that it was beyond the council's jurisdiction.

"Why they are picking on you and your neighbors, I can't possibly tell you," he said. He explained that the rules were not local ordinances, but were State Department of Environmental Protection and Energy (DEPE) rules that were being enforced.[17]

A normal ECRA filing can tie up a business or a transaction for one to five years. Only by detailing the scope of the regulations, costs, studies, work, engineering, and environmental surveys required can one begin to understand the problem that he or she will face in ECRA. (Refer to Appendix 3 for the scope of one's liability under this system.) This does not address the emotional, business, and personal problems that a citizen goes through when put through the "wringer." Since ECRA is legislation that goes against constitutional principles, it feels very unreal when one becomes embroiled in it. One related thread found when interviewing individuals undergoing ECRA is that they are universally angry and feel personally abused.

Two constitutional areas are relevant for review: 1) Section 8, Item 3—No bill of attainder or ex post facto law shall be passed. 2) Amendment IV, the right of the people to be secure in their persons, houses, papers and effects against unreasonable searches and seizures shall not be violated.

One businessman told me, "there has never been a law that is more after the fact than ECRA." A present owner can be forced to clean up property that he owns that was despoiled by others, perhaps before his birth. This pollution could have occurred by following the *legal* or *engineering norms* of that particular time. At the present time in New Jersey, in order to sell, merge, or finance one's business, or even move it across the street, you *MUST* file ECRA. In this process, you must testify against yourself or be forced under the threat of losing your assets to waive your rights. You may have no alternative but to invite "search and seizure" onto your own premises, even though the Fifth Amendment to the United States Constitution states ". . . nor shall he be compelled in any criminal case to be a witness against himself . . . without due process of law, nor shall private property be taken for public use without just compensation."

In order to do business in New Jersey, you must file under ECRA. If you do file you *must* state all that you know about your business and property. (Refer to Appendix 3, Certifications.) If you have polluted, you can be held criminally liable by your own reporting of it. If you lie, you could be criminally liable for perjury. If you tell the truth, you can be fined or penalized for doing so. If you choose to say nothing, you can be fined for nonfiling. Evidently, guarantees against self-incrimination are not considered to be part of the process.

As for "just compensation," it is your money that is used to clean up the sins of others. It's your money that must be used to prove that you are *NOT* the polluter if off-site contamination exists. It's your money that must clean up a mess even if a midnight dumper drops six drums on your property. The "midnight dumper" disappears into the night while the property owner must clean up the mess or face fine and prosecution.

The author is a limited partner in a property that was dumped on for years. The property is fenced in, posted, guarded, and occupied. The partnership, in one case, found out who was responsible for dumping and reported it to the local police who reported it to the proper township detective bureau. But nothing happened to the dumper. Later, under county government order, our partnership spent thousands of dollars painstakingly cleaning up the dumper's waste. The innocent party paid, the criminal profited, and the police didn't react, even though we gave them the garbage owner's address labels from the dumped property.

A New Jersey businessman put it properly when he said: "It's an insane law—belongs in an Eastern bloc country, not in New Jersey!"[18]

One New Jersey businessman who survived ECRA told his story.

> The objective of the law is laudable, however, the reduction to practice is pathetic. If the NJDEPE wants a response

from you, substantial fines are threatened. This is the case if your response isn't received within a short time. If, however, you want a response from them, be prepared to wait for many, many months. After three years and the expenditure of over $35,000, none of which was penalties, the NJDEPE decided that we had no problem and *no clean-up was finally required.*

Our money was spent on environmental consultants, lawyers, and fees. This money was drained from our business that employs over fifty people with annual sales of $4,000,000. Our business was in plastics hence we must have been polluting. Then they went on their three year witch hunt flush with taxpayer money and not caring about our company's money. All of the soil tests around the building came up clean, and within limits. Their response, "this can't be. Let's drill six sampling wells," at $6,000 each. They showed clean, also, no underground contamination appeared. The DEPE response, "this still can't be." Four more wells were drilled, at $6,000 each. Still everything came up clean, as we protested. The whole affair stunk and was appalling. The DEPE people don't get mad, they get even. Our company tried to reason, argue, press our case, show them, etc. We were told, "Don't create problems or we're sure we can find some reason to shut you down." We shut up, and cannot reveal ourselves! Remember: *NO CLEAN-UP WAS EVER RE-QUIRED.*[19]

Another businessman who owned a barrel company and who has gone on record protesting his NJDEPE experiences stated:

Thanks to the DEPE, EPA, RCRA, OSHA, etc. all of which caused over sixty percent of our business volume to leave the city of Newark and the state of New Jersey, Bayonne

Barrel & Drum Company was forced in 1982 to go into Chapter 11 of the Bankruptcy Code—and for the last four years, we have been trying to sell the property. This has been to no avail because of the unrealistic, and, in my opinion, unconstitutional conditions imposed on me by ECRA.

It is not only heartbreaking; it is disgusting. What is even worse is that the bureaucratic sector of our various governmental agencies do not realize what is happening, or they just do not give a damn. When the end results come to roost, we will be in a situation worse than the great depression of the thirties.[20]

Civil libertarians have long believed that two of the greatest threats to our valued historical freedoms were: (1) the ill-fated suspension of habeas corpus by Abraham Lincoln during the Civil War, and/or (2) the roundup of Japanese-Americans during World War II. The current environmental hysteria, however, has once again resulted in persecuting innocent citizens and could qualify for equal blame.

One of our legislators who is trying to correct some of the wrongs in the current approach is Assemblyman Arthur Albohn of Morris County, New Jersey. He states:

No one can really take issue with ECRA insofar as its purpose and intent are concerned. What hurts unnecessarily is the time taken by DEPE, the lack of clarity in the statute and regulations, the retroactivity back to a time when most people could not even spell "environment," and the assignment of guilt against even the most obviously innocent property owners.

We do not need and do not want a repeal of ECRA. What we do need is a rewriting of the statute so its language is unequivocal and clear, and a provision for the clean-up of sites without bankrupting the present owner when he is clearly innocent of any wrongdoing.[21]

Hopefully, efforts like those of Arthur Albohn's will become law and replace the current regulatory nightmare.

II

What is the ECRA Virus?

It will come as a surprise to most people when they learn that in New Jersey, the populist anti-business, anti-growth, policies began with the Republican administration of Governor Thomas Kean and with a *Republican controlled state assembly*.

Under Republican Speaker Chuck Hardwick's tenure, New Jersey passed dozens of superb sounding bills such as: Environmental Clean-Up Responsibility Act (ECRA), the New Jersey Right to Know Act, and the Clean Water Act. These and other bills resulted in the creation of paperwork nightmares, long delays, increased costs, unfairness, and heavy fines for business operating in the state. None of these regulatory nightmares operated as advertised, and all caused significant grief to the business communities affected. As indicated herein, a recent survey showed that ECRA causes a business applicant to spend 80 percent of required funds on paperwork (lawyers, filing fees, etc.) and only 20 percent on clean-up. Longstanding liberties were also not considered by the legislators.

The "Environmental Clean-Up Responsibility Act" (ECRA) was signed into law on December 31, 1983, by Governor Thomas Kean. Kean wished to be remembered as an environmental and education governor.

But the Governor had apparently insulated himself from the difficulties this legislation caused. The author sent six letters to Governor Kean protesting the law, its regulations, and its persecution of innocent New Jerseyans. One letter was answered about a year after it was written and was quoted in Chapter One. Its most memorable line was "Please note that although ECRA does *require the current owner* to clean up the site, this does not preclude that party from pursuing legal action through the courts."

This letter, dated June 9, 1988, was considered a triumph as no one else could get answers on this subject. It was found out later that critics, such as myself, were shut out of his office.

Three months later, at a meeting with New Jersey DEPE officials, Lance Miller, then acting head of ECRA (now head of ECRA) said, "Bruce, did you get my letter?" "What letter, Lance?" "Why, the governor sent your complaints to me, and I wrote his letter. It was then signed with the office mechanical signing pen." That ended any hope of ever reaching Governor Kean.

As James Sinclair of the New Jersey Business and Industry Association, a 12,000-member trade group in Trenton, put it, "Big Brother is in the middle of the real estate transfer process. They may have perestroika in Eastern Europe, but it hasn't touched New Jersey yet."[1]

Thomas Kean signed the ECRA law, but its father was Raymond J. Lesniak, a Union County democrat. He believed that ECRA would set a precedent. He predicted that ECRAs would spread to many states in the country. That prediction has proven to be untrue as the chart on page 27 shows. Senator Lesniak stated that "this is going to be the most important legislative tool that the state has to clean up hazardous wastes."[2] When Senator Lesniak authored this unfortunate bill, he, like others, mistakenly believed it would have a very narrow application. Supporters, at that time, did not believe that the New Jersey DEPE would make a cruise missile out of a pea shooter. ECRA's far-reaching powers, however, have the ability to literally plug up any and all economic transactions, under misty legal foundations.

ECRA's spread to other states has been halted by the extremely negative New Jersey experience. Other states have limited environmental reporting requirements and have kept state government out of oversight in their "ECRA-type" laws. Connecticut, Iowa, California, Oregon, and Washington State now have such laws, and the Illinois Responsible Property Transfer Act took effect in January, 1991. Legislation is pending in New York and Pennsylvania while eleven other states are soon to consider it.

"The New Jersey experience has most states wary of adopting an ECRA clone," says Vicki Masterman, an environmental attorney with Jones, Day, Revis & Pogue, in Chicago. "You can maximize public disclosure on the environment without stopping all business transactions through the funnel that ECRA has become."[3]

STATE PROPERTY LAWS OF ECRA TYPE
As of May 1, 1991

California—Effective 1988
•This is a Disclosure Law. Seller must notify buyer of hazardous materials beneath the property.

Connecticut—Effective 1987
•Requires a Disclosure with Negative Declaration or Clean-up Plan and schedule for implementation.
•State can impose Priority Lien and initiate clean-up if voluntary compliance does not occur.

Delaware—(Proposed 1991)
•Requires Disclosure to Buyer with Negative Declaration or Clean-up Plan.

Illinois—Effective 1989
Responsible Property Transfer Act
•Requires disclosure of environmental condition on a state filed questionnaire.
•Requires disclosure to buyer, lender, county recorder, and state EPA.
•Either party can cancel if disclosure reveals previously unknown problems.

Indiana—Effective 1989
Responsible Property Transfer Law
•Requires disclosure of environmental conditions to buyer, and lender.

Iowa—1988
Groundwater Hazards Statement
•Requires disclosure document to be given to buyer covering areas of potential environmental impact.

Michigan (Proposed Environmental Response Act)
•If passed, this would require a disclosure document for environmental conditions, would give the state a priority lien for environmental clean-up. This law would give an innocent landowner protection from clean-up liability.

New Jersey—Environmental Clean-Up Responsibility Act (ECRA) 1983

New York—(Proposed 1991)
Property Owner Protection Act
•Would require a site assessment.
•Would require certification that no release has occurred on site. It would also require a certification which states the owner is committed to cleaning up the site.

Oregon—Environmental Clean-up Law 1988
•Applies to facilities defined by CERCLA CFR 302.3.
•Defines liability pursuant to CERCLA/SARA.
•Incorporates Innocent Landowner defense.

Washington—Citizens Initiative No. 97, 1989
•Defines clean-up liability pursuant to CERCLA/SARA.
•Incorporates Innocent Landowner defense.

What Is ECRA?

ECRA is the acronym for New Jersey's "Environmental Clean-Up Responsibility Act." The law was designed to prevent the sale, transfer, or abandonment of contaminated industrial real estate. The regulations are administered by the NJDEPE's Division of Hazardous Waste Management.

In simplest terms, ECRA mandates that as a precondition of the closing, sale, or transfer of an industrial property, owners must file an application to determine whether that property is subject to clean-up. If a negative declaration is filed and approved by the state Department of Environmental Protection and Energy (DEPE), the property owner is home free. But if it is determined that clean-up is needed, the problems can be overwhelming. The cost of soil sampling is usually significant. Actual clean-up costs mean more expense for the owner and/or operator unless the purchaser voluntarily assumes the responsibility. In that case, the purchaser must be granted "permission" to do the honors by the DEPE.

There is an initial three-part test to determine if a particular business is an "industrial establishment" subject to the rules. First, ECRA applies to the industrial establishments that are classified under Standard Industrial Classification code number groups. Second, the business in question must have been involved in the generation, manufacture, refining, transport, treatment, storage or handling of hazardous substances or wastes on the site, either above or below the ground. The third condition is that the property or business is either being sold, closed, or transferred. There are two ways to get through the ECRA process. The first is by making a simple declaration that the property has been cleaned or doesn't need to be cleaned. The DEPE will review the statement and, if everything seems in order, grant approval. Case closed. Unfortunately, the process has been expanded to where it isn't as simple as it sounds.

The other way is to come up with a mutually agreeable plan between the DEPE and the current property owner or operator to clean up the site. After determining that the site needs cleaning, a schedule of clean-up, to be completed over a period of years, is devised and approved by the DEPE.

Conforming to ECRA regulations has become so confusing that the Applebaum Realty Group Inc. of Lyndhurst, N.J., an industrial and commercial real estate brokerage firm, recently devoted an entire issue of its newsletter to explaining ECRA to potential clients.

"As a New Jersey resident, I'd love to see the state cleaned up," says Howard L. Applebaum, the firm's president. "But as a broker, I see it as a lot of bureaucratic red tape that has slowed the transfer of title."[4]

The law appeared to be pioneering and precedent setting when first enacted. Since enactment, however, due to very wide NJDEPE interpretation, overreaching regulations, and broad bureaucratic application, ECRA has become a detrimental business regulation act with wide-reaching effect in many direct and indirect areas.

ECRA was in the vanguard of the national "clean-up mania," along with other federal and state sister proposals. Taken together, these ideas formed "the birth of a new religion—"environmentalism."

As Ronald J. Brandmayr, Jr. wrote in the Newark, N.J., *Star Ledger:*

Like any religion, its dogma transcends science and requires a leap of faith. Scientists who challenge its suppositions and misconceptions are branded heretics. There is no room for debate, compromise, or dissension.

The Clean Air Act is a product of this environmental hysteria. Ten years ago the environmental demon was the coming Ice Age. Today the demons are global warming and acid rain. Just when American industry seems to have regained its competitiveness, it is smashed with new regulatory policies that will increase production costs so severely it may, according to some economists, render us incapable of competing in international markets.

But facts are the first casualty of ideology. No congressman wants to be the guy who voted against "clean air."[5]

ECRA may also be used to define a type of thinking process. Extremists can always justify legal excesses if they have a good cloak. By maintaining that one is "protecting the environment," the opposing side becomes totally disarmed. Opposition, by definition, becomes anti-environment. Hence, "ECRA thinking" can steamroll opposition and justify extremes because it is cloaked by environmental protection. People, property, and legal rights can be pushed aside because the high sounding goal takes precedence over annoyances like freedom and individual rights. The "ECRA thought process," similarly, permitted the internment of Japanese-Americans during World War II. The word "environment" was simply exchanged for the words "war effort."

What Is The Fee Structure?

ECRA's fees and costs are considerable. If one files under ECRA, he faces large out-of-pocket expenses. These costs can include: (1) outrageous state filing fees; (2) site surveys; (3) engineering/consulting; (4) legal; (5) laboratory and testing; (6) approved environmental removal contractors; and (7) miscellaneous related expenses. Filing fee requirements are listed below:

Normal Fee	Activity	Small Business Fee
	Initial Notice Review	
$ 2,000	Without a Sampling Plan	$ 750
$ 3,000	With Sampling Plan with UGT analysis. No GW monitoring	$ 1,500
$ 5,000	With Sampling Plan	$ 3,000
$ 7,500	With Sampling Plan that includes GW monitoring	$ 4,500
$ 1,000	Sampling Plan Data	$ 1,000
$ 500	Negative Declaration Review	$ 250
	Clean-Up Plan Review (Based on Cost)	
$ 1,000	$1 – $9,999	$ 1,000
$ 2,500	$10,000 – $99,999	$ 2,500
$ 5,000	$100,000 – $499,999	$ 5,000
$ 8,000	$500,000 – $999,999	$ 8,000
$11,000	Over $1,000,000	$11,000
	Clean-Up Oversight Plan (Based on Cost)	
$ 1,000	$1 – $9,999	$ 1,000
$ 3,000	$10,000 – $99,999	$ 3,000

Normal Fee	Activity	Small Business Fee
	Clean-Up Oversight Plan	
$ 7,000	$100,000 – $499,999	$ 7,000
$10,000	$500,000 – $999,999	$ 10,000
$12,000	Over $1,000,000	$ 12,000
	Other	
$ 200	Applicability Determination	$ 200
$ 300	Deminimus Quantity Exemption	$ 300
$ 500	Limited Conveyance Review	$ 250
$ 2,000	Administrative Consent Order	$ 2,000
$ 500	Amendment to ACO	$ 500
$ 350	Confidentiality Claim	$ 350

For complete details, see Appendix 5.

How Is ECRA Triggered?

The scope of business transactions which trigger ECRA compliance was limited in the law, but in practice became very broad. ECRA was originally intended to regulate "the sale of closing of industrial establishments." But the current scope of ECRA goes far beyond the original law and its intent. As with so many environmental regulations, it has found its way into a host of uncharted and unforeseen areas. The NJDEPE, consultants, and lawyers have created a formidable network of spider-webbing. In the background are related promulgations from the federal EPA, Army Corps of Engineers, counties, and cities, etc.

Some of the non-buy and sell events that can trigger ECRA are:

a) Death of an owner, or control person.
b) Bankruptcy, in certain circumstances.
c) Going public (because of change in ownership, control).
d) Selling adjoining pieces of property, even if the property is virgin land. While a 20 percent exemption exists for the sale of attached vacant land, it has rarely been permitted.
e) A general partnership that owns or operates an industrial establishment where a minority partner sells his interest.
f) Sales of subsidiaries (including L.B.O.s back to the original management).
g) Mergers.
h) Takeovers—the purchaser becomes "strictly liable without regard to fault" for ECRA compliance.
i) Moving a business to another New Jersey location, even across the street.
j) Taking in new partners, i.e., selling a portion of the business.

There are so many real and potential ECRA triggers that they are now ingrained deeply into day-to-day management decision-making of all New Jersey business. These triggers have reached out-of-state companies, since the NJDEPE has gone after parent companies and related parties for satisfaction of their demands. As a businessman stated very well: "The lawyer's fees and costs of inspection were excessive. In addition the paper work was terrible. We were declared "clean" in September 1989. We are in the process of another transaction that has triggered the ECRA process, again. Despite the declaration in September, the entire paper process will start all over at a cost of many thousands of dollars."[6]

ECRA applicability is based in part upon property use. The current use of the Standard Industrial Classification (SIC) system for determining ECRA applicability is what the law requires. However, this applicability is very inconsistent. ECRA regulates such clean industries as sewing and basket weaving shops, yet exempts junkyards, chemical research testing laboratories, dry cleaning plants, gasoline stations, and other businesses that handle significant quantities of hazardous substances. ECRA exempts auto and truck repair businesses, yet regulates motorcycle and forklift truck repair businesses. Warehousing of finished products is regulated by ECRA if conducted by a manufacturer, but usually not regulated if conducted by a wholesale distributor. As with most environmental regulations, the aims can be fuzzy and the results agonizing for the permit seeker.

There are many common problems encountered by applicants in completing the ECRA forms. For example, on the site (SES) map the applicant must indicate paved vs. unpaved areas, or the map is considered incomplete by the NJDEPE. Neither the regulations nor the instructions to the SES specifically identify the need for this information. In the site-history section of the application, it is often difficult or impossible to fully or accurately account for all property uses since 1940. While property ownership records are available, property use records generally do not exist. Hence, older properties present a substantial and unfair burden to the owner when preparing an ECRA application. Property owners can be held responsible for the sins of their predecessors going back to the 1700s, when environmental risks were unappreciated.

If an application is deemed incomplete, a minimum case processing delay of three to four weeks results—an exasperating situation for an applicant making his best efforts to comply. Once a delay pattern begins, it usually compounds to another and another.

ECRA filings can tie up a business or transactions for one to three years. Only by reviewing the scope of the engineering and environmental surveys required can one begin to understand the problems. Unfortunately, most business loan transactions cannot survive in the application stage for more than 90 or 120 days.

The NJDEPE has taken the original ECRA concept and law and has expanded it into a noose that encircles all it snares. So much power results from the filing of an ECRA case and the promulgation of regulations that the results are mind-boggling.

Excessive regulation, over-burdening costs, delays and enormous paperwork can be the same to a business transaction as incarceration is to an individual. Imagine having the ability to write regulations without legislative oversight (New Jersey has none) and then enforce whatever it is that you write. Next, if the company doesn't obey your doctrine, you can fine them and conduct appellate hearings within your own organization. The first light of day seen in this process occurs only when you appeal to federal court. But few have the money, time, or fortitude to do this. The result of environmental overregulation has become a crushing experience to its recipients.

The NJDEPE is also involved in Orwellian misspeak. They explain what they are actually doing so that all pronouncements sound socially necessary and plausible. That individuals are being unfairly coerced, is rarely made public. One attorney refers to ECRA as "The New Jersey Environmental Extortion Act."

Judith Yaskin, former commissioner of the NJDEPE, wrote an article in the Newark N.J. *Star Ledger,* specifically answering some of this writer's complaints. Read casually, her answer makes sense; read deeply and carefully, it is frightening in what it says and doesn't say:

> Siminoff takes DEPE to task for the Environmental Clean-up Responsibility Act (ECRA). Such resistance to ECRA is not new. At the same time, other states have come to New Jersey to find out more about ECRA because they are interested in creating a similar law. ECRA places financial responsibility on owners of industrial sites to clean up contamination before a property transaction can proceed. It is a valuable tool for ensuring that when an industrial property is sold, transferred or closed down, environmental problems aren't passed along as well.
>
> This law makes sense. Those who cause pollution should pay to clean it up, not New Jersey taxpayers. Industry doesn't like that idea. But New Jerseyans don't like it when a contaminated property is passed along from owner to owner until one day we discover a significant health threat to nearby neighbors. We only have to look to the chromium problems in Hudson County to find an example of such a dubious legacy.
>
> It is true that ECRA clean-up regulations are still being developed. We are addressing a longstanding need for these regulations going back to previous DEPE administration. The fact is that many companies cited for ECRA violations have failed to supply sufficient information or properly no-

tify the DEPE that an industrial property is being sold or closed down. The notification requirements are clear. Industries across the state regularly follow them. DEPE expects all owners of industrial properties to follow them.

The New Jersey envisioned by this administration is one where businesses can grow and develop in a way that doesn't threaten the environment and health of the people who live here. DEPE's goal is to make sure New Jersey is a place where commerce and clean air and water share the same environment. It would seem that from Siminoff's view that would make good business sense long into the future.[7]

The commissioner tries to make bureaucratic sense out of gross injustice. When language and overbearing regulations can be used to enslave a populace, then one must stand back and view the forest as well as the trees. Today, laws, rules, and regulations can subvert the Constitution, the Bill of Rights, and can take any businessman's property (by regulatory and/or fining power) without due process, or a fair hearing. Appealing through the court system against a bureaucratic agency is not a practical answer since it can bankrupt all but wealthy persons or large firms. This destruction of citizen and business rights seems to be permissible if it masquerades as improving the environment.

Commissioner Yaskin's defense of these complaints sound very plausible on the surface. Her reply is, unfortunately, simply a surface response. Commissioner Yaskin says, referring to ECRA, "this law makes sense. Those who cause pollution should pay to clean it up, not New Jersey taxpayers. Industry doesn't like that idea." The truth is, industry has never said that. ECRA doesn't work at all in practice as Commissioner Yaskin and its proponents state that it does. It operates in an unfair, unconstitutional, and unjust manner. Under the rules, *the polluter doesn't clean up—the present owner cleans up!* Ask yourself the following questions:

- If a real estate broker took a one-half of one percent as a commission interest in a general partnership, under NJDEPE regulations he is stuck within ECRA. He can't sell, transfer, or even give away his shares. Is he the *responsible party* for environmental clean-up?

- If a person owns a property that is now an office building, but which once was an industrial site, polluted one hundred years ago—he gets ECRA and can be totally wiped out financially by previous pollution of the property, which occurred without his knowledge. Is he the *responsible party?*

- If a bank, mortgage company, or leasing company lends money to a company that fails and goes bankrupt, the lender gets ECRA by becoming the new owner. Is the lender the *responsible party?*

- If a tenant moves out in the middle of the night, "stiffs the property owner for the rent," breaks the lease, pollutes the owner's property, and flees to another jurisdiction, the innocent property *owner* gets ECRA. Is the owner the *responsible party?* Did he pollute the site?

- If a company is going through an ECRA case and its property is being polluted from somewhere else (say, a mile away), they are not only stuck with the clean-up, but can be rendered a pauper—and victimized by someone else's pollution. It can be incumbent upon the applicant to *prove* it's not his pollution, monitor the pollution and in some cases, even clean it up! The person in this case is the *victim! Is the victim the polluter?*

- If you own waterfront property polluted by the tides, you can never survive ECRA. But you are nevertheless responsible. If your building is built on fill dredged up one hundred years ago, as it was along the Hudson River, you can't clean it up. NO ONE CAN. ECRA can destroy you and your business for previously legal back-filling, done before you were born. Is the victim in this case the *responsible party?*

- If a city takes over a distressed property via a tax lien, it must ECRA the property. Our older New Jersey cities have assumed ownership of hundreds of buildings in this category, and can be pauperized in the process. None of these cities has the financial ability or expertise to ECRA these sites. Hence, many of these properties have become abandoned, are in disuse, and in some cases have been taken over by the homeless or by drug users. Why is the city the *responsible party?*

These are just a few examples of the horrors that ECRA has caused the economic climate, our business community, cities, and citizens. ECRA in its regulations and its execution has compromised our traditional system of justice, constitutional processes, and sense of fairness. It does not work in practice the way Commissioner Yaskin stated. In practical terms the implementation of ECRA regulations has doomed many of New Jersey's older industrial cities to rival the economically abandoned "South Bronx," section of New York City.

Let's examine the NJDEPE regulations and their ramifications as their effect on the financing of New Jersey business, real estate development, and their impact on New Jersey property values (commercial and industrial).

Yaskin goes on to state: "Siminoff blames overregulation by NJDEPE for curtailing the development and financing of business activity in New Jersey. This is a remarkable statement."

But truth is remarkable. Industrial development, expansion of plants, and new manufacturing starts are *in reverse.* New Jersey continues to lose manufacturing jobs at a remarkable rate because of the misapplication of environmental regulations.

As this book is written, industrial real estate is in a virtual depression. Vacant factory buildings populate the state and have become valueless. Owners of old buildings are trapped by ECRA. Owners of new buildings are afraid to rent to ECRA-subject manufacturers due to the NJDEPE's stance on secondary pollution liability. Lender liability prevents mortgage companies, lessors, and banks from financing new projects. This problem is found under ECRA as well as federal EPA regulations. Why is financing so difficult? Because a bank can lose its loan plus additional unforeseen dollars if it has to foreclose on a business or property. Under NJDEPE's implementation of lender liability (as well as certain federal rules), *the present owner has to clean up a property,* so when a bank or city (pursuant to a tax lien) forecloses on a given property, they become the new owner!

In New Jersey the innocent present owner cleans up—not the actual polluter!

ECRA makes a mockery of individual rights under the disguise of environmental protection. Most businessmen favor a clean environment but not by draconian measures. Consider the spirit (and the letter) of the law of our justice system that ECRA attacks:

1) Since ECRA is self-funded it assesses filing fees that can total $20,000 in a sizable case and $10,000 for a medium-sized case. Because of the size of the filing fees (more than a court fine for many misdemeanors), one can reasonably conclude that they are punitive—without the right of appeal. Pay the fee or you are fined for nonfiling! ECRA fees are required to be paid by businessmen or property owners—not by virtue of their wrongdoing.

2) Because of delays in getting through ECRA, one to four years, the right to one's private property can be abridged without the opportunity of legal protection or court review.

3) If you are a landlord or tenant, you are "pinned in place" during the process. You can't move your business, can't substantially repair the premises, and can't rerent the facility until the case is cleared. If a landlord or tenant has a three-year lease, can either party wait one to three years to move or rerent the facility? A tenant daring to rent a building currently going through ECRA puts his economic life on the line. He can

become jointly and severally liable! Who would take that chance while there is a surplus of buildings available for lease?

4) Most ECRA-subject businesses and property owners are no longer able to obtain mortgage financing for their businesses or property. The bank or lender inherits the possible clean-up costs if forced to foreclose on the property. While the property may or may not be currently clean, who would lend to a business or property owner only to inherit unknown future clean-up costs and delays?

5) If a company is forced to go bankrupt, their right to do so is abridged by ECRA in several ways. First, ECRA supersedes other debts. Second, if the company is unable to fulfill its obligation, then the NJDEPE may attempt to hold the trustee in a bankruptcy proceeding, the assignee for the benefit of creditors or a state-appointed receiver who signs the ECRA filings or an ACO responsible for ECRA compliance. People assuming this role can be liable for clean-up and removal costs and damages, without limitation. Such parties can be required to furnish the same information and otherwise be responsible as any other owner or operator.

Do you know any individual, executor, conservator, or attorney who would accept an assignment where he may become personally liable for his client's (or descendants') clean-up responsibilities? Why is a trustee or advocate responsible for the acts of his client?

6) ECRA jeopardizes the ability to will property to some-one other than one's own family. This is because the clean-up costs and regulatory requirements are passed along, if not willed to one's family. As the new current owner, the recipient picks up the liability. If one's property is ECRA-subject, it is no longer his own, it can only be deeded with state approval, which as interpreted, can be nearly impossible. What happened to the right of private property?

7) ECRA is cloaked as "environmental clean-up," but its regulations reach deeply into the day-to-day decision making of labor and management. For example, if a company sells more than 50 percent of its cash assets or investments, it can trigger ECRA! If a person who controls 55 percent of a public company sells 6 percent, ECRA can be triggered to impact the share-holders of the entire company. The innocent outsider shareholders could now be frozen in their tracks by diminished values. If a company owns several subsid-iaries and sells or moves one of them, the parent company can be tied up by ECRA. The result is that headquarters companies will have to leave New Jer-sey—or any state that adopts these policies—because they can't comply. If they did comply, they wouldn't be able to buy, sell, close down, or open any business, affiliate, or subsidiary. Such regulations jeopardize shareholders, employees, and management.

8) ECRA punishes the innocent. If a tenant leaves waste on a property, the landlord can be responsible for the clean-up. If a landlord has waste on a tenant's location,

the tenant can be responsible. If trespassers or vandals "dump" on your property—and if you complain to the police—you have to pay for the clean-up and filing costs as if the innocent were the guilty party. In many states you are required to report illegal dumping under penalties of fine. If you are unfortunate enough to own property where a polluted stream runs through it or a drum was buried thirty years ago by somebody else— that's right—it's your problem!

Any time a government forces a sector of its populace to clean up someone else's mess under duress, the people will respond. In this case ECRA, which was designed to "clean up New Jersey," will clean out New Jersey. It will do the same to any state adopting these abrasive measures. If another state or Federal EPA were to pressure manufacturers, owners, assemblers, or processors in this unfair manner, those affected would move elsewhere, perhaps to South America or the Far East. Business and jobs (even clean office buildings housing headquarters companies) will go elsewhere where they are perceived as wanted.

We can coexist in a society where the environment is protected, but it is also necessary that its laws remain unpolluted. In our society citizens should not be held responsible for two hundred years of pollution by our ancestors. Americans are unwilling to tolerate totalitarian-like rules and regulations. Our society must not abandon its justice system, including the abrogation of rights against self-incrimination and the abuse of search and seizure protections.

ECRA is environmental extortion, the simple extortion of citizens by inappropriate government regulations.

III

Caught in the Agency's Web
Without Regard to Fault

Simple words that have been written into environmental regulations can be chilling when exposed to the light of day. These can be relatively simple traps to very complex ones. For example, Regulation 7:26B-1:13 states that a person must sign the following affidavit to enter the self-incriminating system of ECRA:

> I certify under penalty of law that the information provided in this document is true, accurate and complete. I am aware that there are significant civil penalties for knowingly submitting false, inaccurate or incomplete information and that I am committing a crime of the fourth degree if I make a written false statement which I do not believe to be true. I am also aware that if I knowingly direct or authorize the violations of NJSA 13:1K-6, et seq, I am personally liable for the penalties set forth at NJSA 13:1K-13.

Let's examine this requirement. First, ECRA is a program involuntarily entered. If you own an old building, can you honestly state what has occurred there for fifty, one hundred, or one hundred fifty years previous to your ownership? *Do you know whether former employees spilled solvents in the rear of the building?* Do you know if a former tenant buried drums? The word "knowingly" can place you in a complex legal dilemma.

Throughout the patchwork of environmental regulation is the continued feeling that one is denied his fundamental right to "due process of law" guaranteed to every United States citizen. The due process concept is part of the 14th Amendment to the United States Constitution, which bars any state or local government from the deprivation of life, liberty, or property without due process of law.

The following definition is offered by Black's Law Dictionary (6th edition, 1990):

> Due process of law implies the right of the person affected thereby to be present before the tribunal which pronounces judgment upon the question of life, liberty, or property, in its most comprehensive sense; to be heard, by testimony or otherwise, and to have the right of controverting, by proof, every material fact which bears on the question of right in the matter involved. If any question of fact or liability be conclusively presumed against him, this is not due process of law.

The definition of the simple word "knowingly" in the ECRA regulations is vexing to an honest petitioner. Does a current owner enjoy "due process" if he must attest to all uses since the industrialization of New Jersey in the 1700s? But that's what he must do as the current owner.

What is the result of forcing a current owner or business to undergo possible penalties and personal liabilities so that they may clean up two hundred and fifty years of someone else's mess? It's an easy answer for big business. They can knuckle under once and then move away to other states or countries. The small and medium-sized companies are caught in a steel trap, even if innocent.

Keystone Camera Case

When caught in the ECRA or regulatory snare, the results are always predictable. The little guy is the one who is hurt. Note the problems that terminated one of the last United States camera makers, Keystone Camera Co. Unfortunately, Keystone had various financial problems and filed Chapter 11 in 1991.

Another company tried to save the business and the jobs. Unfortunately, ECRA and its regulations worked in reverse. They provided hardships that could not be overcome by small or medium-sized companies. Hence, as the following article in the Bergen County, N.J., *Record* recounted, any chance of saving the company was destroyed by these regulations.

> Concord Camera, which recently bought the equipment of bankrupt Keystone Camera in Clifton, said Monday it has scrapped plans to reopen the shuttered plant and hire back about one-third of the five hundred workers who lost their jobs when Keystone closed in March.
>
> Concord of Avenel, which bought Keystone's equipment during Bankruptcy Court liquidation in May, said environmental problems at the site quashed plans to reopen the plant.

"If we started to manufacture there, we would inherit and potentially be liable for clean-up of any and all environmental problems that exist there," William Pearson, Concord's executive vice president, said Monday.

"We were looking for some way of operating there, but we can't take the liability," he said.

When Concord bought the bankrupt Keystone's machinery, its officers said they wanted to resume manufacturing of at least one line of cameras at the factory and rehire about 150 of the company's laid-off assembly workers.

As part of the liquidation of Keystone and transfer of its assets, the state Department of Environmental Protection and Energy ordered an environmental assessment and clean-up of the property, a normal requirement under the state's Environmental Clean-Up Responsibility Act (ECRA).

But Pearson said Concord, which didn't buy the land or buildings at the Keystone site, doesn't want to inherit any problems that might be missed in the current assessment and clean-up. Under state law, it could be liable for any future clean-up if it operated on the site.

Some 500 production workers, along with close to 200 administrative workers, lost their jobs when Keystone closed down in March.

Kevin Nolan, a local Teamsters union officer who represents the 500 production workers, said Monday that most of them are still unemployed.

"It's a vicious economy out there; there aren't many production jobs," Nolan said. "We were all very excited for awhile.[1]

The impact of voluminous and costly ECRA compliance requirements will continue to impact plans of many businesses with operations located in New Jersey. Over time this will influence employment and restrict industrial growth, as it did in the Keystone case. More importantly, in New Jersey and elsewhere, manufacturing firms will continue to move to where they are welcome. If this means relocating out of the United States, they will do it.

Allen R. Wood, who is in charge of real estate for the Westinghouse Electric Corporation, commented about ECRA.

> ECRA is probably the most stringent environmental law in the whole country as far as selling or buying real estate. I've heard of several big companies who have shied away from the state [N.J.] because of the law. Westinghouse has several cases pending with regard to vacating property that are just tying us up in knots. In one case we've had a buyer lined up for two years but we've been waiting all that time for the clean-up plan to be approved.[2]

Mr. Wood informed this writer that as of August 18, 1991, the above reference was outdated. Westinghouse had then been involved in ECRA four years.

Some large companies have spoken out, while some others have simply "spoken with their feet," and are quietly planning to leave. A subsidiary of NYSE is listed as "I.C. Industries," and is now committed to the sale or moving of all four of its New Jersey operations. Adverse and costly environmental regulations were the reasons given for this relocation of their facilities.

Additionally, "Figgie International" said in a letter to its stockholders in the company's 1986 Annual Report, "This corporation, and I presume others, will never locate any future operation in states like New Jersey . . . and will immediately relocate any new acquisitions, if they occur, from these types of states." Figgie International, Inc., a Fortune 500 company based in Connecticut, spent fifteen months trying to sell a New Jersey plant while complying with ECRA requirements.

What the company didn't say is that the ECRA virus started in New Jersey and has spread to only a few other states (See Chart, State Property Laws, Chapter II). Some states have followed in broad concept only. The closest sister to ECRA on a national basis is "Superfund," which is also a costly failure (see Appendix 3).

This bizarre turnabout of American justice has created hosts of horrors. To be the person caught in this web, saying "I didn't do it, I'm innocent" doesn't matter. Even if you prevailed with this argument (in federal court), the cost of the victory and travail could break you. The NJDEPE, the New Jersey Assembly and Senate, and the executive branch of state government doesn't appear to exhibit any concern about the rights of New Jersey citizens. They just don't care! In numerous meetings with State officials it's always the same answer. "We'll look into it and try to correct some of the excesses." But no corrections ever arrived. The siren song of the environment with its reelection melody has stilled the voice of justice. Justice has been clouded by a host of extremists ringing doorbells. Justice has been further stilled by the enormous fining power of the DEPE.

Many companies will not publicly speak out because of adverse publicity, fear of increased pressure from state or federal agencies, or premature disclosure. Early discussion of plant closing could run afoul of various rules, both state and federal. The author has had opportunities to speak with several New Jersey manufacturers about the state's business environment. Of six firms interviewed, three have taken steps to curtail some of their expansion or to sell their New Jersey operations. One of these firms, a large organization, will reduce employment in New Jersey by more than five hundred jobs over the next three years. New facilities will be opened in the South, Southwest, and in Europe. While none of these firms agreed to be identified publicly, each mentioned "overbearing environmental regulations" and/or increasingly punitive regulatory conditions as a key factor in the decision to relocate away from New Jersey.

> ECRA has become a bureaucratic process aggravated by the legal system. Testing is expensive, redundant and excessive. Consultants are getting rich quick, and businesses suffer the costs. New Jersey is as effective in its ECRA legislation as it is in Auto Insurance. Briefly, the personnel are poorly trained, unreasonable and unconcerned about cost, time delays or inconvenience. ECRA should concentrate on the major polluters, who do not intentionally trigger ECRA by avoiding all of the mechanisms which necessitate ECRA involvement.[3]

A small New Jersey firm, Polychrome Press of Princeton, learned about ECRA the hard way. They simply tried to sell their business to a prospective purchaser. David O'Johnson, the owner, wrote an article about his experiences.

> New Jersey's ECRA was lying like a sleeping giant athwart the state's environmental statutes. It appeared to awaken the moment my company, Princeton Polychrome Press, started final negotiations for its sale to a major New York magazine.
>
> We initialed preliminary papers for the sale in December 1984 and then approached ECRA for the permission needed to make the sale. It had to be done that way, since the law will not allow you to start getting ECRA approval in anticipation of selling at some future, indefinite date.

New Jersey has taken this law a step further and requires that, before they can be sold, companies with certain SIC code numbers must first get permission from the ECRA Bureau. The EPA number for printing and chemical companies is Code #27. The fine for selling, without permission is $25,000 a day, plus other penalties, including nullification of the sale itself.

We were first made aware of the basics of ECRA at about the time we were signing the contract to sell. We were also warned that, since it was being administered by a new agency, it might take two months to complete the few tests which seemed to be required for a letter stating, "By this approval, the New Jersey Department of Environmental Protection and Energy (NJDEPE) hereby waives any right to void the referenced transaction pursuant to N.J.S.A. 13:1K-13(b).

The sale of our company hung on that one, crucial sentence.

We signed our contract to sell on March 6, 1985, and set the closing for July 15, 1985, at 10:00 a.m. in New York City.

All seemed well.

How foolish we were to think that!

The way things turned out, in the convoluted process of proving to ECRA administrators that we were not contaminating the environment, not only was the sale aborted but we nearly lost the company because of the sheer dollar drain of that $240,000 in expenses as well as the unconscionable drain of management time and energy.

As we studied our situation, we knew there was no way for a business of our size to delegate responsibility for compliance negotiations. And so—between early March and the 15th of July, 1985—the compliance process took almost the full time of both the president/sales director and vice president/manager. Sales and production suffered, employee morale slipped, forward motion was slowed. Little surprise that, after five months, the company books were no longer in as favorable a condition as when the deal for the sale was signed.

Now to the procedures which proved so costly to our company.

The first procedure involved completion of a five-page form—"ECRA I"—[Appendix II] that must be submitted to the Bureau of Industrial Site Evaluation within five days after public notification of a decision either to cease operations or to sell.

Questions pertain to the company's previous ownership, location, industrial classification number, use of public sewage treatment resources, proposed date of sale or termination, and any environmental actions that may have been filed against the firm in the past ten years.

After agency approval of ECRA I, you can then proceed to "ECRA II," which is more complex.

1. A scaled site map identifying all areas where hazardous substances or wastes have been generated, refined, stored, handled, or disposed, above or below ground;
2. A detailed description of operation, with particular attention to the handling of hazardous materials such as ink, photo chemicals, processing materials, wash-up solutions and fuel oil;
3. Types, age, etc. of storage facilities;
4. Leak tests on all underground tanks;
5. Description of any spills;
6. A detailed sampling plan which includes proposed soil, ground water, surface water, surface water sediment, and air sampling determined to be appropriate for the site, and
7. Copies of all soil, ground water and surface water sampling results, including effluent quality monitoring, conducted at the site of the industrial establishment during the

history of ownership by the owner or operator, including
a detailed description of the location, collection, chain of
custody, methodology, analyses, laboratory, quality as-
surance/quality control procedures, and other factors involved in the preparation of the sampling results.

After ECRA I approval, and in consideration of requirements of ECRA II, we proceeded to hire an engineer. He, in
turn, engaged a testing laboratory to take certain soil samples
through test borings around our building, and then to make
laboratory tests of them.

As it turned out, although the engineer was on a state-
approved list, he had not done an ECRA before. Nor had the
testing laboratory he engaged. As an example, the first price
we got for a hydrostatic test on our 400-gallon fuel oil tank
was $4,000. We finally got the test done correctly, with the
approved affidavit, for $400.

The results of those first tests were catastrophic:

First, the samples were not taken in accordance with
ECRA's latest and everchanging requirements.

Second, they were taken in bottles with plastic tops, which
altered the true condition of the soil samples and thus invali-
dated the tests.

The result was five weeks of wasted time, money, and
effort, plus the necessity of getting new soil samples taken
and analyzed by a new laboratory, supervised by a new
environmental engineer, and then coordinated by a new lawyer with extensive environmental experience.

The new tests supposedly showed very high levels of
hazardous chemical compounds in the various soil samples.
We had never knowingly used some of those compounds. At
that point, we did not know their tolerance levels in parts per
million—and, indeed, we found out later that no particular
standards existed for some of the chemicals we were required
to test.

In other words, to some extent, the NJDEPE was setting standards as we went on our quest for approval—and all New Jersey standards were continually higher than the federal standards. It seemed that the standards were whatever the new and changing technology could test for!

By this time we had six weeks left before our July 15, 1985, closing date for the sale.

After consultation with our new, environmentally experienced team and with representatives of ECRA, we realized it would be virtually impossible to complete all the procedures and tests in time. But, we also realized that the only thing we needed was a letter from the NJDEPE giving us permission to sell. So, we decided to "go for it."

With six (6) weeks in which to accomplish what we finally realized was twelve (12) weeks' work, we set about to meet the closing deadline. If we did not gain the approval in time, we would have to bear the costs of the ECRA compliance and also have to return a $200,000 downpayment.

Basically, what we needed was to have test borings done all around our plant—a building of 22,000 sq. ft. sitting on approximately four acres. It was determined from the test borings that ECRA had three areas of concern:

(1) Our old septic field, which had not been used for four years.
(2) The underground fuel oil tank, which we had replaced three years before and had relocated approximately ten feet from the previous tank, and
(3) A lagoon area which we had cleaned up approximately three years before at the request of the DEPE at a cost of $24,000. (The finding then was "non-hazardous waste which can be dumped in any sanitary landfill in the State of New Jersey.")

Now to Item (1), the unused septic field.

Approximately five years ago, when we had neither city water nor city sewer, the DEPE was concerned that our plant might be polluting the wells of the neighboring residents, so they conducted tests on all the wells involved and found no contamination. Yet, even though we were not polluting five years ago when we were using the septic system, and even though we had not used it for four years, we still had to prove we were not polluting the water table. In the intervening years, we had hooked into the local sewer authority and they had checked our discharges periodically and found no problem.

In spite of that history, in order to prove our present innocence, we had to have two new wells drilled on our property. Findings verified that we were—and still are—O.K.

The cost of that verification was approximately $34,000.

Item (2), the underground fuel oil tank, also proved costly.

The underground soil samples showed unacceptable levels of hydrocarbons on one side of the new tank. Hydrostatic tests had proven there was no leakage from the present tank. Therefore, the previous tank had leaked, or, in removing the old tank, some No. 2 fuel oil had been spilled, and fuel oil is considered a hazardous waste. It was admitted there wasn't a lot, but, in the final disposition, we had to remove a couple of truckloads of soil and ship it in sealed containers to a hazardous waste dump site outside of New Jersey.

Cost: over $16,000.

Item (3), the lagoon, had a bit of environmental history, to say the least.

In 1960, when we were considering the building site for our plant, there was no city water or sewer. We had asked the Township authorities where we could discharge our film processing waste water. They had pointed out that there was a quarter-acre lagoon on the site, and, since it was next to the Township Sanitary Landfill, they gave us the O.K. to discharge into it. The lagoon's overflow connected with a drainage ditch from the Sanitary Landfill.

We discharged our photographic wash water into the lagoon for nearly 19 years. It was the home for frogs, salamanders, and for two turtles which grew noticeably larger as time went by. During this entire period, we were recovering the silver from the photo wash water.

About six years ago the NJDEPE came around in answer to a complaint that we were discharging dark substances from our plant and that they were draining onto neighboring property. Negotiations about that lasted somewhat over a year. At one point the state was threatening to have us store all our wash water in large tanks, and then we were to ship the water in approved, sealed tank trucks to a north Jersey processing site at a cost of approximately $2,500 a month.

Neither our tests nor those of the state agencies ever proved the presence of any hazardous materials in those discharges, but the black color of the sludge seemed to bother the technicians, who continually monitored the wash water and the water in the lagoon. Basically, the color was partly due to the decomposition of leaves from the trees surrounding the lagoon, and partly to the inert silver sulfide left over from our processing. All the while, drainage from the adjacent Township Sanitary Landfill area seemed of no concern to the state authorities, since three quarters of the lagoon was on our property.

In the end, we agreed to remove the sludge from the lagoon area and bring in clean fill. About the same time, the Township waters and sewers were connected, and the Division of Solid Waste Disposal gave us approval to dispose of the now admittedly nonhazardous sludge from the lagoon in any sanitary landfill in the state without a Hazardous Waste Manifest.

After a state-guided clean-up that expensive, we figured our lagoon site was free of problems.

Not so.

The fact that one agency, in this case the Division of Water Resources and the Solid Waste Administration, had approved the site in April of 1982 meant nothing as far as the ECRA division was concerned. They determined that not all of the sludge had been removed in a manner that conformed to the new standards, so we had to re-dig a good portion of the previous lagoon area, take many more tests, and ultimately refill with uncontaminated fill dirt.

Cost of that operation: $66,000 over and above the $24,000 spent in 1982.

Here's the tally so far:

Item (1), unused septic field	$ 34,000
Item (2), underground fuel oil tank	$ 16,000
Item (3), the lagoon	$ 66,000
Laboratory Testing Fees	$ 48,000
Engineers, Lawyers, Accountants	$ 76,000
Total	$240,000

As things turned out, after all the surprises and aggravation, all the rush and worry, we managed to get the ECRA approval with two hours to spare.

By then, however, not only were we out of money and out of heart but another party had unexpectedly purchased the magazine which wanted to acquire us. Had we been able to get the ECRA approval within two months of that purchase, the sale would have been consummated as planned. With the additional two and a half months to chew on the situation, it was decided that Princeton Polychrome Press did not "fit" the new owner's plans. We arranged a financial settlement to help with the clean-up costs, but this in no way covered the momentum lost by our business in the interval.[4]

Another printing firm that ran into similar NJDEPE diffi-culty was D & M Reproductions in Dover. The President of D & M, J.H. Crafferty stated, "With the burdensome appli-cation process, New Jersey is a less inviting place for small businesses affected by ECRA."[5]

Mr. Crafferty's problems reflect the difficulties that most printers have with ECRA. Users of inks, solvents, press wash, and cleaners may have been totally unaware of the stringent regulations regarding the disposal requirements for many of these substances. ECRA is not "grandfathered"— hence, disposal practices of previous years (prior to 1983), are now being viewed retroactively and are currently vigor-ously enforced by the NJDEPE. The environmental damage that had been previously done is in reality everyone's prob-lem, and should be solved on that basis. Retroactive enforce-ment is not the answer to the solution of any environmental or societal problem, especially if people were unaware of the harm at the time they took the action.

On a broader basis, what about the millions of dollars of potential environmental clean-up liabilities that are "off the balance sheet" of many public companies. Shouldn't shareholders be told about them? These items affect a stockholder's investment without his knowledge of their existence. Off-balance-sheet liabilities of New Jersey com-panies include: (1) long delays in completing deals (1-3 years); (2) use of the New Jersey environmental laws as an anti-takeover device (the company initiating the takeover picks up the environmental responsibilities in New Jersey;

(3) the practical reduction in net asset values of process equipment, buildings, etc., which now may have a *reduced residual value* (this can be below book value) because of having been "contaminated" environmentally; (4) the inability of subject companies to obtain bank financing due to joint and several lender liability as well as subordination of future claims, even if the banks don't foreclose; (5) perpetuation of management due to ECRA, which can be triggered onto a company by certain changes in management or their shareholdings; and (6) industrial facilities using premises that are twenty years old or older have the added liability of *NOT KNOWING* what is in the soil, in the rafters, under the roof, or perhaps buried in the rear. As we have said, in New Jersey the present owner pays, not the polluter, hence, the present innocent owner may not know what is there. This unfair process keeps management as well as shareholders in the dark, and presents fertile ground for lawsuits.

As previously stated, ECRA can make today's innocent present owners the victims of their predecessors past environmental mistakes. Once found in this position and under current regulations, which clearly state "without regard to fault," the owners may have no other alternative than to take their problems to the courts. NJDEPE regulations don't recognize innocence as an excuse. Their regulatory position is generally stated. If it's on your property it's your responsibility to clean it up, regardless of when it was put there. If one doesn't prevail in the courts, then he must bear the financial burden.

A case in point recently occurred in Hanover Township. Since the present owner is responsible, complicated court cases are commonplace. They go down a chain of previous owners catching all in their web, innocent or guilty. Since the

ECRA regulations were not grandfathered, the following strange and convoluted situation occurred:

> Ziff Communications Co., a publishing firm with property in Morris Township, has sued a Parsippany printing business and related companies that previously operated there, charging they dumped hazardous wastes on the site.
>
> The suit was filed with the Morris County Clerk's Office yesterday against L.P. Thebault Co., company president Louis P. Thebault and three affiliates—Dorsey Co., C.R.C. Corp. and Boniface Printing Co.
>
> It alleges the contaminants have burdened Ziff with the cost of state-ordered studies and clean-ups and resulted in the termination of a proposed sale of the East Hanover Avenue site to Redwood Press Inc.
>
> Dorsey, according to the suit, sold the property in 1980 to Ahl Computing Inc., which Ziff Davis Publishing Co. of Delaware purchased in 1982 and transferred to Ziff when the company reorganized in 1986.
>
> The suit says the property was used only as editorial offices and for warehousing books, magazines and floppy discs after Dorsey sold it.
>
> The suit contends that while Thebault and related companies occupied the site between 1956 and 1980, they discharged hazardous wastes into a cinder block cesspool in violation of township zoning ordinances and state pollution laws.
>
> Ziff contends it discovered the pool and contamination and that the pollution leaked into surrounding soil in 1985.[6]

The above case is only one of a host of retroactive, complicated court filings involving litigation being spurred by unfathomable regulations. There is a Southern New Jersey case in which the seller is suing the purchaser who is suing to defend himself, while the occupant (neither of the above) is suing regarding his lease. The problem is that the short-comings of after-the-fact application of environmental liability as well as the law's convoluted regulatory web are creating fertile ground for a multitude of suits and court proceedings. This confusing result benefits no one, jams the courts, and causes an unnecessary level of anger and frustration by all parties.

In Appendix 2, an article appears regarding the Federal EPA Superfund Program. In a broad sense the Superfund is the big brother to ECRA. Referring to this article will show the reader that in one Superfund case, nearly 300 law suits have been filed. When this occurs, it's the law that must be wrong, not the plaintiffs and/or the defendants.

Unconstitutional deprivation of one's property can occur in many forms. This can be as simple as a substantial bureau-cratic delay, enforcing fees that one can't afford, or making mountains of paperwork that you can't economically or prac-tically accomplish. ECRA and many other environmental regulations contain all three components. The filings can be so complex, so burdensome, so technical and so patently ridiculous that many people caught in the web are driven to financial insolvency. I was a member of a committee that was ushered into an office of an irate ECRA internee and shown a wall of bound volumes. "Our company's case has dragged on for over four years and cost five times what it should have," according to the company spokesman.

In order to retain his sanity (easily lost by those persecuted under the cloud of environmental hysteria), the businessman put the "ECRA" books in a measured pile along his office wall as kind of a "Count-of-Monte-Cristo" measured re-sponse. Each book had been measured by inches, which had then been converted to pages. As the businessman piled them up, he could easily add the total pages. He labeled this data along the wall. The nearly final paperwork (four years of it) then measured nine feet high. The businessman stated that there were additional tests to accomplish and estimated that twelve feet of paperwork would result by the time his project was completed.

Taking a conservative average (depending on weight) paper runs about 250 pages to the inch, or 3,000 pages to a foot. This company's ECRA filings had subtotaled 27,000 pages, and the estimated completion number was to be 36,000 pages. The time required, energy expended, and expenses created seemed to him to resemble the Spanish Inquisition, except he viewed it as mental, not physical torture. Ask people who have been caught in this malaise. They all say the same thing. "I don't know how to get out of it, it keeps going on and on and on!"

Another businessman reported that "it makes no sense to me to say a company is guilty of contaminating soil and water from years and years ago when there were no environmental laws, no disposal procedures, no safety data sheets, no warning labels and no right to know. . . ."[7]

Equally galling, but to a smaller degree, is the substantial required state filing fees, which are charged every time one submits any paperwork. Every time an applicant makes a move in his ECRA travail he incurs large costs; filing fees, lawyers, consultants, engineers, testing labs, etc. This travail can only be unscathingly survived by the largest companies. The NJDEPE has literally set out to wipe the state clean of small and medium-sized businesses, since most simply can't afford the ECRA fees or the process.

Once caught in ECRA, small business has few practical options. They usually must try to "muddle through" or try to wend their way through the two or three year difficult regulatory maze. Large business can post performance bonds, just comply, or like "Figgie International" pay the price once and take their facilities elsewhere.

A dental products manufacturer, located in Southern New York State, maintained a small storage building in New Jersey that was rented to an unrelated individual for warehousing. The individual, it turned out, rented many locations under a legitimate business guise. He and his associates actually used the locations to collect and store hazardous wastes illegally.

The group was caught and subsequently jailed for their criminal waste collection activities. The dental company (the victim) cooperated in every way with the authorities. Management related to me that the police complimented them for their assistance and found that they had been duped by the crooks, as were their customers. The crooks had provided everyone with official looking receipts and disposal manifests that were quite convincing. In reality, of course, they pocketed the cash and just stored the waste products. They never disposed of them in the manner which they had promised.

The NJDEPE, however, ordered the dental company to rid the premises of the stored hazardous wastes. After all, the dental company *had become the new owner of the illegal wastes,* since they owned the building. The victim protested, but the NJDEPE stated that if they didn't clean it up, they would be held corporately and personally liable for storage of hazardous materials. This liability would enure to officers and directors. As the owners of the building they were "jointly and severally liable, without regard to fault" even though they were the victim of an elaborate swindle.

The costs of removal approached $300,000. While the process is three-quarters complete at this writing, the company has nearly been pauperized and been made insolvent by the crime effected against it. As an added insult, in order to then sell the building in the future, ECRA will be then triggered, since "hazardous wastes were once stored there." Once again, the victim will pay.

In the 1986 RCA-GE merger the NJDEPE threatened to hold up the impending change in ownership of the New Jersey operation until the companies complied with ECRA. Since the combined companies possessed twenty-six New Jersey facilities, there was no way in which an ECRA process could be completed in order to permit a timely consideration of the merger by the public shareholders. Hence, GE-RCA agreed to post $36 million in financial guarantees to assure the NJDEPE requirements.[8] GE and RCA combined are the fifth largest employer in New Jersey; and while they were able to post a bond of this size, few smaller companies have the resources to do so, or could even consider this option. Even if a company could post the bond, many buyers or lenders will not agree to close a deal until ECRA has been completed. Business planning then "freezes" pending completion of the process, which in most cases takes years. This puts New Jersey businesses at a disadvantage with their out-of-state competitors and makes the state a less inviting prospective home for new manufacturing businesses.

It is thus reasonable to conclude that no business caught in the ECRA web or having completed an ECRA experience, would *want to try it again!* Most businessmen will only admit this privately, hence the following anonymous statement: "We purchased our company from a large corporation.

They paid all the ECRA expenses. I can't believe or imagine how a small company [could] afford to pay such costs."[9]

Another effect of retroactive environmental rules is their affect on state and local planning. An unnecessarily difficult ECRA regulatory (or environmental) program clearly works against the idea of state master planning. While a master plan would most likely encourage redevelopment of inner cities and old industrial areas, the opposite is usually the case. For example, a developer facing retroactive environmental rules in an old factory neighborhood has three things working against him: (1) higher costs; (2) considerable time delays; and (3) a host of historical, technical, and bureaucratic unknowns. When compared to the problems potentially faced in old inner city areas, it is much cheaper, easier, and safer to develop open virgin farmland. The practical facts of ECRA compliance work to destroy the idea of revitalizing old industrial cities, hence, ECRA will defeat this aspect of master planning by its contrary rules and regulations.

Joseph R. Douglass works full time on ECRA and environmental compliance issues for Environmental Waste Management Associates. Mr. Douglass spent five and one-half years as a Supervisor of Case Managers for the NJDEPE ECRA program. According to Douglass, the single biggest problem with ECRA is the enlarged size of the program. "Too many small and clean properties are regulated," says Douglass. Some contain less hazardous material than the average house. To start, ECRA requires historical descriptions of property uses back to 1940, detailed site maps, a minimum of six to eight notarized signatures per application, certified checks or money orders, and much, much more. This paperwork can be a nightmare when trying to sell a multi-tenanted industrial building, even when there are no major environmental concerns. And while NJDEPE spends a great portion of its limited resources reviewing and processing these "low environmental concern" cases (60 percent of the ECRA caseload), the applicants with real environmental problems experience substantial delays.

Douglass further states:

> The Legislature would be doing a great service to both the business community and to NJDEPE by adjusting the applicability focus of ECRA using more environmentally sound criteria. This would allow NJDEPE to concentrate on the properties truly warranting environmental investigation and clean-up . . . the remaining properties would not be ignored.
>
> The recent developments in State and Federal environmental law have greatly increased the general level of environmental awareness in the business community. In today's market, if ECRA does not apply to a sale, a private environmental audit is routinely conducted at the insistence of the buyer, the buyer's attorney, or the lender. The investigation and clean-up is performed to current ECRA guidelines. These guidelines, and the increased level of environmental awareness, have certainly been the most positive effects of the troubled ECRA program.[10]

A Newark *Star Ledger* article of May 29, 1988, quotes Patrick J. O'Keefe, Vice President of the New Jersey Builders Association, on the redevelopment difficulties caused by ECRA:

> The ECRA phenomenon has complicated efforts on the part of developers to get projects going in the cities.

"Often, when a buyer looks at vacant parcels in urban areas, he finds they had a prior use that puts them into the ECRA system," O'Keefe pointed out.

And the "mere possibility" of contamination puts the transaction into the ECRA process," which he calls extremely cumbersome.[11]

While redevelopment of cities is a major state problem, another large difficulty can be found in coastal, riverfront, or tidal areas. The cost of the proposed clean-up of land abutting any major polluted waterway is tremendous, and the ability for a private individual to effect the clean-up is nearly impossible. These property owners are faced with a real catch-22. Owners along polluted sections of the Raritan Bay, Hudson River, and Newark Bay may be faced with an inability to comply with ECRA's requirements. They didn't cause the pollution and have no control over the tidal effects on their properties. Until ECRA and the attitudes it engenders are changed or relaxed, inner city redevelopment along with tidal improvements cannot be economically pursued.

Senator Gerald Stockman, of Mercer County, was quoted as saying: "We have to make sure that the worthwhile state effort to clean up past mistakes does not jeopardize our long awaited urban renewal investment needed to turn around the major cities."[12]

An additional and unnecessary problem arises from the NJDEPE's hard-line methods of handling its cases. Many businessmen have reported that NJDEPE has been confrontational rather than cooperative, creating a difficult environment and sending negative vibrations throughout the business community. As Richard S. Beltram, President of

Intedge Industries, aptly stated in a letter to the editor of the *Business Journal of New Jersey:*

> Our firm ceased manufacturing in the state in early 1990. Although we prospered in 1987 and 1988, the New Jersey state government pulled the plug on manufacturing in 1989.
>
> As a recipient of a tremendous government burden, we moved to South Carolina. Labor rates are essentially the same. I would suggest a lobbying effort to dismantle the anti-manufacturing sentiment in New Jersey before it is too late . . . the last one leaving the state please turn off the lights.
>
> I feel very depressed to have to write this letter but after being a lifelong resident of New Jersey and having my grandfather found the firm in the state in 1914, I feel that the same government is flirting with very serious circumstances that will [affect] New Jersey residents for generations in the future.[13]

The attitude of any governmental administration has much to do with its success. Careful and judicious writing of regulations is critical to compliance. Constituent cooperation is paramount to the success of enforcement. The following article appeared in the Morris County *Daily Record* on Thursday, December 15, 1988, and shows how well-intended rules and regulations subjected to hard-nose enforcement can backfire:

DEPE FINES FORCE HIGHER SEWER RATES

A rate increase for sewer and water customers of the township Municipal Utilities Authority was approved by the utilities board Tuesday night.

Water rates will rise 6 percent and sewer customers will pay a yearly $480 charge, $80 more than this year. The new rates take effect January 1.

Sewer fees increased because of a $30,000 fine levied by the State Department of Environmental Protection and Energy, said MUA Chairman William Morris. The MUA was fined for not meeting standards for treated water discharged into Stoney Brook.

The fines means the MUA will post a deficit for the fiscal year, but money from the new rates will be used to upgrade the treatment plant to meet DEPE standards.

While the above is not specifically an ECRA case, it nevertheless goes to the heart of the environmental enforcement attitude, the ECRA thought process. Punitive actions that, in essence, "fine" innocent homeowners or business property owners will only continue to inflame the issues. Why does a state agency fine a Sewer Authority, which simply passes the cost on to innocent homeowners? Proper management to clean up the environment should develop from the formation of partnerships. These partnerships must be developed between the NJDEPE, cities, corporations, sewer authorities, etc., *to clean up New Jersey.* They must be forged so that clean-up proceeds in a fair and equitable manner for all concerned.

It's not just confrontational behavior that is of issue, but the predictable overall results. A mindless bureaucracy breeds a negative business attitude. A survey of more than one hundred New Jersey government officials, industrial real estate agents, and bankers conducted by Dr. Donald Merino, a professor of management at Stevens Institute of Technology in Hoboken, in cooperation with the Hazardous Substances Research Center in Newark, found strong agreement that ECRA lowers the employment rate. "The conclusion was that ECRA has had a major negative impact on such variables as property values, employment and retail sales, particularly in urban-industrial areas," said Merino.[14]

In June of 1991, this writer received a letter from Ed Croot, a realtor with offices in Warren County, New Jersey. The letter is reprinted in its entirety and speaks for itself:

> Three years ago I was sitting on the top of the world; I was the most active industrial real estate broker in Warren County, and I owned several industrial properties myself. Today, I'm in deep trouble. I don't know if I can survive!
>
> Under ECRA regulations, it's virtually impossible to sell a piece of industrial real estate in New Jersey! One of my clients, a sweet, innocent . . . lady whose uncle left her three industrial buildings, two of them in Hackettstown, wished to sell her property. I listed them, and within sixty days put both properties under contract with qualified buyers, who were ready to close. The 15,000 sq. ft. building was contracted at a price of $300,000 and the 20,000 sq. ft. building was listed at $375,000; both went to contract in May/June 1986. The larger building closed because the seller was able to post a $500,000 bond to guarantee clean-up and comply with ECRA. On the second building she has spent almost $400,000 with lawyers and consultants in five years! But, the NJDEPE has not even approved a clean-up plan! In one case it took the DEPE sixteen months to respond to information submitted to them!
>
> The estate is drained! There's no money left! The woman was under unbelievable stress for four and a half years. She's now under doctor's care and is no longer executrix of the estate! One of the buildings is vacant; the building is deteriorating; windows are broken! The property is being used as a dump.

In February, 1986, I put a 13,500 sq. ft. manufacturing building under contract in Somerset County. The owner's attitude was, *"whatever the law is, I will obey it!"* The property was under contract of sale for three and a half years at a price of $925,000, and because ECRA took so long, this deal fell through! It took four and a half years and over $300,000 to get through ECRA, and now all the owner has is a vacant building and no buyer! The only ECRA problem discovered after four and a half years was oil-stained soil. They took out thirty loads of dirt at an unbelievably expensive price of $1,500 per load to an ECRA approved dump.

One client, who owns three manufacturing companies in New Jersey, promises he will never locate another plant in this state.

One major corporation in Warren County wanted to donate a large building to the county college. But, they elected to tear the building down instead, to avoid having to deal with ECRA.

The regulations are destroying industry in this state; they're destroying manufacturing capacity; they're throwing thousands of people out of work, and, they are doing little to clean up the environment. What they are doing, is making the lawyers and consultants rich!

They use buzz words like "hazardous and toxic" to create alarm! The environmentalists rave about the birds, save the fish! But, they are destroying people's lives! Thousands of businessmen, workers—have been put through hell! They have taken hundreds of good buildings (and thousands of jobs) out of circulation. They are destroying our economy, all in the name of clean-up. And, the only ones cleaning up are the lawyers and consultants![15]

Unfortunately, abusive regulations tend to become more abusive. What is the next step beyond fines? The answer is:

"Let's teach a few lessons. That approach should scare the rest."

We are reputed to be a democratic society held together by laws and a reasonable judicial system. But when bureaucrats have been granted significant powers, and see only the correctness of their cause, then severe consequences will ensue.

Flagrant polluters are not the only ones at risk. Various environmental rules contain many onerous provisions that even the best-intentioned companies are likely to violate. Prohibitions in the New Jersey Clean Water Enforcement Act, for example, obviously include intentional violations of effluent levels in discharge permits. But an executive whose company fails to submit a discharge monitoring report in any two months of a six-month period is also termed to be a "significant noncomplier" and may face *criminal,* as well as *civil,* consequences. Stiff *minimum* penalties are mandatory for *criminal* noncompliance; they cannot be negotiated down.

Certainly, there is precedence for individuals, including high-level managers, to be found guilty of crimes, which they did not personally commit under such traditional theories as aiding and abetting a conspiracy. Recently, however, the "responsible corporate officer" doctrine has been utilized in environmental cases to prosecute managers whose jobs merely bear a "responsible relation" to the activity that caused the violation. The Third Circuit has recently held that knowledge of illegal action may be inferred from the position held by a defendant within the corporation. Judges have employed jury instructions that would make authority and power to control, without having exercised that power to prevent or even to discover a violation, the basis of a conviction. *Bottom line: a corporate officer can be found guilty if he or she does not even know that a violation has occurred.*[16]

Imagine, in ten short years we have developed into a society that can put someone in jail even if "he or she does not even know that a violation has occurred." Under the "joint and several liability" doctrine you can be brought into a civil penalty position (and possibly criminal, later on) if someone else (your tenant, borrower, deceased husband?) commits the stated offense.

Concern for the environment has been elevated to a level that supersedes our constitution, our sense of justice, fairness, and common sense! As one businessman told me plaintively: "There used to be two things certain in life—death and taxes. Well, under ECRA, a small business owner can't even die. A new disease, ECRA, follows the owner into the grave."

IV

Environmental Hysteria and You

The pendulum swings, often too far to either side. The ECRA pendulum, however, has not reacted as normal pendulums do. Pollution is a danger to all of us in the United States, but like all issues it must be addressed on a rational basis. The present response to cleaning up the environment has entered a phase of "irrationality," and if the federal and state tempo continues, negative consequences are a certainty. Fairness is out the window, justice is in tears, and innocent peoples' lives and assets are in jeopardy for environmental crimes they have not committed.

Business is being hammered by ECRA, sewer authorities are being fined by the DEPE, red tape is entangling everyone, and dozens of laws are being passed under the banner of a cleaner environment—except that fairness and positive results are being caught in the crossfire, a catch-22—and if you dare to speak out against it you are labeled "anti-environment." It is time for the pendulum to swing back to the middle when we can have a clean environment, a pro-business attitude, and legislative sanity. The environment has spawned much controversy, and here are some cases in abject irrationality.

Litter Reversal

The state's anti-litter program has buried itself so deeply in paperwork, regulations and complex contracts that cities and towns are reluctant to accept grants offered for clean-up projects.

As a result, the state, with $11 million in the bank, has distributed only $350,000 under the Clean Communities Act because municipal officials say they can't deal with the bureaucracy in the New Jersey Department of Environmental Protection and Energy (NJDEPE).

"We decided not to apply," said Peter Braun, the township manager of Randolph in Morris County. "Based on what they published as requirements for administration and record-keeping, it was just so onerous. The bottom line is that it would cost us more than we would get.

"We figured we could get $25,000. We went through the procedures and both our health officer and assistant manager threw up their hands and said in order to get $25,000 it would cost us $40,000."[1]

A citizen writes his lament to *The Star Ledger,* as follows:

Red Tape Tangles Housing

Since January of last year I have been trying to build a house on an existing lagoon in Bayville. This is an existing development, one of the last lots left. The lot was graded and bulkheaded years ago. The redundancy of paperwork has been amazing, not to mention $3,000 worth of fees and engineer's reports.

Governor Kean says the bureaucracy needs to be reduced, but in October he signed legislation that has caused so much delay and added so much cost to my house.

I'm not looking for a profit but I think it might be easier to build in Russia![2]

Result: The environmental bureaucracy has caused the price of housing in New Jersey to soar and pulses of homeowners to rise. Long-term results will be neither a positive labor/business climate, nor a cleaner environment. Another citizen voices his concern about the small operators of service stations:

New Gas Tank Rules Will Force Stations to Close

Brace yourselves, motorists and gas station owners, not only in the Garden State but across the continental U.S.A.

Why? Well, the ultra-environmentalists, so well documented in Rael Jean Isaac's book, "The Coercive Utopians," are again on a roll. This time they're planning to "legally" force out of business an estimated one-fifth of the nation's gas stations by employing the code words: "new environmental safety rules."

According to the Petroleum Marketers Association of America on January 30, the upcoming gas station closure law would probably not put the squeeze on gasoline supplies, but would, particularly in rural areas, force up prices and make motorists drive farther to fill up and to get their cars repaired. Ah, yes, the average American loses again.

The regulation by which these radical environmentalists intend to wipe out one-fifth of the nation's gas stations mandates that the owners of underground petroleum storage tanks, such as those at retail gas outlets, furnish proof that they can pay any and all damages in the event their tanks leak.

In their zeal to return us, unrealistically, to a once pristine wilderness, the utopians are costing average Americans a mint.

"I don't think anybody can deny that gas stations contribute to pollution. But they're hitting us, especially the little guys, with everything all at once," said Jerry Ferrara, executive director of the New Jersey Gasoline Retailers Association.

Add up the costs of compliance with all these different regulations, and we're talking as much as $200,000 for a (gas station operator) small businessman. Pass it on to the customer and you're talking an extra ten cents a gallon, which means major oil retailers will kill us.

Don't be surprised if the mom-and-pop stations just close their doors and walk away. We're talking the end of the neighborhood gas station.[3]

Yes, service station owners will lose their businesses and car owners will lose their local service. Wouldn't cooperation and education help to solve this problem? Mandates seldom work. Why force the small businessman out? Can't it be done another way? Are heavy fines for paperwork violations the answer? Recently, *The Star Ledger* reported that:

The Federal Environmental Protection Agency (EPA) yesterday proposed fining three New Jersey firms more than $66,000 for violations of the Resource Conservation and Recovery Act.

A spokesman for Schering-Plough, which the (federal) EPA proposes to fine $8,750, blamed what it called a "minor infraction" on a third-party contractor who used an incorrect code number on waste transported from its Bloomfield plant.

The spokesman said the charge, received by the company December 30, is being reviewed.[4]

Surely an $8,750 fine is not justified for a paperwork infraction or an incorrect code number. If the company's position is correct, it shows the environmental regulator's zeal is to issue fines, not to clean up our environment. Does a heavy fine policy really benefit the environment?

Item in the Chester, N.J., *Observer Tribune:*

Polluting Cars Can Be Reported

Citizens can report air-polluting vehicles to the N. J. Department of Environmental Protection and Energy (DEPE) at (609) 292-7172 or David West, Acting Chief, Bureau of Transportation Control at (609) 530-4035. All reports will be investigated by the DEPE staff.

The DEPE will require the license plate number of the vehicle, date, time, road or street name, nearest cross street and the direction the smoky vehicle was traveling.[5]

Here's a good way to take out your frustration on your neighbors, enemies, or maybe the wife of a local cop who gave you a parking ticket. The NJDEPE might award a free "Vigilante of the Year" T-shirt to each snitch. Will a clean environment result from turning in our neighbors to the DEPE? Is vigilantism the answer?

Here is an example of the DEPE assessing excessive fines:

The State Department of Environmental Protection (DEPE) yesterday levied a $686,000 fine against Perth Amboy stemming from its operation of the Runyon water treatment plant in Old Bridge.

The fines, which were handed down in Trenton, were assessed for violations of the state Water Pollution Control Act, according to James K. Hamilton, assistant director of the DEPE enforcement office.

Hamilton said Perth Amboy has established a consistent record over four years of not meeting several provisions of the Water Pollution Control Act, ranging from excessive effluent to impermissible levels of iron and other solid contaminants in the wastewater.

City Attorney, Robert P. Levine, said Perth Amboy will oppose the fines and request a court hearing.

"Yes, there is iron content. We don't deny that.We may have reasons for it. One of the problems was that we used to be able to cart some of this away, but then the order came that it could not be used as a carpet over the landfill," Levine said.

The DEPE is also authorized to assess an additional penalty of not more than $50,000 for each infraction each day the violations continue, according to Hamilton.

Hamilton said the fines the DEPE is seeking could not be eliminated through bankruptcy proceedings.[6]

The environmental enforcers have proven that they can use their "fining power" in a truly big way. Perhaps a different tack could benefit the sewer authority and its customers. After all, who are the customers of the sewer authority but homeowners like you and me. The illogical effect of this fine is who pays the $686,000. If upheld, businesses and homeowners, "the sewer users," pay.

ECRA is actively engaged in chasing business from New Jersey. In an article in McGraw-Hill's *ENR* in 1989, other businessmen relate their experiences:

"The impact of ECRA is overwhelming," says Nicholas BeRose, vice president of Langan Environmental Services Inc., an Elmwood Park, New Jersey, firm that has handled many of the site audits.

BeRose contends that while some ECRA audits take only six months and cost less than $10,000, others have grown into major financial headaches for owners, particularly when clean-ups may be extensive. "Some ECRAs have cost as much as $10 million," he says. "We have one case that's been going on for five years."

One engineer quips that for many firms, ECRA has come to stand for "Environmental Consultants Retirement Act."

But the measure also has cost New Jersey millions in new development and hundreds of new jobs, claims Jim Sinclair, Vice President of the New Jersey Business and Industry Association. He notes that in one case, an industrial seller incurred $1 million in penalties from the buyer while waiting for an ECRA approval. The multi-national corporate purchaser ultimately built its factory in Singapore.

"It's absolutely insane to put the government in the middle of the transfer of real property," Sinclair says. "If we want to invent a policy that's anti-urban, we're doing it here."

ECRA "is wreaking havoc on the industrial real estate market," adds Michael Francois, director of real estate development for the New Jersey Economic Development Authority. Only its status as a state agency allowed the authority to expedite ECRA approval for part of the $500 million development of the former Campbell Soup Co. manufacturing site along the Camden waterfront, he admits."[7]

The NJDEPE is turning the screws on business. Using rigid rules and unbending regulations, it is driving business from the state. And if the same is done nationally, business will move out of the United States. These businesses are our employers and taxpayers. The result can only be lost jobs, reduced tax revenues, reduced levels of manufacturing, and loss of freedom.

Because of this impossible enforcement policy even innocent homeowners can be fined indirectly by paying higher sewer taxes. A case in point is Roxbury Township that is protesting a $900,000 DEPE fine "for failure to comply with a July 31 deadline to submit upgrading plans." The penalty will ultimately by paid by the homeowners of Roxbury. Their only offense was to have sewers!

In periods of hysteria, your offense can be just being there. As stated in *The Star Ledger:*

> "We are not going to pay the fine," said Councilman Henry Crouse Sr. "We never received correspondence from the state and (we believe) we were only three days late."
>
> The township was notified of the fine by the state in a letter Monday. The township was informed that the design plans were submitted 138 days past the deadline.
>
> The township is under orders from the state to upgrade its sewer plant to meet requirements under the Clean Water Act.
>
> "Roxbury has spent $36,000 on sewer plans," said Councilman James Julian. "We are working to comply with them and we are slapped with a fine."[8]

New Jersey's Vigilante Program

No talk about hysteria is complete without a discussion of New Jersey's newest vigilante program. Think of environmentalists on white horses, armed with long-aerialed cellular phones, charging down the hillsides to protect us. But are we to be protected by a non-expert civilian cavalry who do not know steam from pollutants, algae from green paints, or humus from oil-soaked dirt? We can easily turn neighbor against neighbor, business against business, and the psychotic old lady on the hill against the nasty old farmer in the valley. We can do this by dialing "1-800-NJ CLEAN." New Jersey has placed in service an 800 number to receive calls about environmental miscreants. This may be a politically sound move, but it does not bode well for creating a free law-abiding atmosphere. It simply fosters ill will and distrust.

As this book is being written, an even more terrifying process is being debated. It's called the "Hazard Elimination through Local Participation Act," or HELP. New Jersey HELP can be termed the "Son of ECRA." The same thought process, which does not respect individual property rights, due process, or the ban against ex post facto legislation converged for the birth of New Jersey HELP.

During periods of mass hysteria all of these ideas begin somewhat quietly. As they gather steam, it becomes evident that the promoters desire more than is stated on the surface. Their real plan has got to be deeper, because anyone who cares about democratic institutions could not participate in these thought processes. The thinking behind New Jersey HELP is absurd!

Legislation which Assembly Speaker Joseph Doria has called "vigilantism in parts," was set to be released from committee in December, 1990. The New Jersey Hazard Elimination through Local Participation Act (HELP), A.2832, was supposed to have been modified to meet the many valid complaints about it by business and libertarians. However, despite assurances to the contrary, the HELP Act remained virtually unchanged, and wormed its way out of committee.

Assemblyman Robert Smith of Middlesex County has admitted that the bill is radical in that it would allow workers to shut down plants on mere suspicion of a health hazard and would require employers to let environmentalists, community activists, and union representatives to inspect their facilities and documents at will, without prior notice, even if trade secrets would be revealed. Assemblyman Smith, however, deems the legislation necessary, and organized labor has made the legislation a top-priority item. Speaker Doria had vowed to have the bill on Governor Florio's desk by April 1991 for his signature, but he didn't make the deadline.

New Jersey HELP would transform the federal Right-to-Know law into a powerful, pervasive, and intrusive "right-to-act" role for workers, unions, and environmental activists. The proposed law, which has bipartisan support from dozens of legislators in the Senate and Assembly, would permit various groups to participate in day-to-day business decisions and operations.

Local Emergency Planning Committees (LEPCs), which were originally created by the federal Right-to-Know law, are composed of local public officials, doctors, labor unions representatives, environmentalists, community activists, and the press. These committees originally were permitted to search a plant for hazards without notice several times per year. Under the federal Right-to-Know Act, however, these citizen groups would have to petition the courts for a warrant to do so, even though their searches still do not have to be announced to the company. While the federal law offers the protection of court intervention, the proposed New Jersey law does not.

Further, the HELP Act would create additional groups called Qualified Community Organizations (QCOs) with similar inspection powers. While the QCOs and LEPCs are limited to searching a single facility once every quarter, there is no limit to the number of groups that may be formed to monitor one facility. Thus, it is not inconceivable that a plant could be subject to uninformed search parties roaming their facilities several times a month! These searches would be conducted by inexperienced citizens who might have any conceivable grievance against an employer or property owner. These searches would not be protected by court intervention unless the company were able to obtain a "cease and desist" order.

In addition to the possible disturbances caused by these inspections, a company would also be required to pay costs associated with the operations of the LEPCs, including any special training or equipment needed to make an inspection or experts required to analyze tests. Copies of meeting notices, minutes, and documents will have to be provided by the business on demand and must be kept for thirty years.

Special jobs would be created by HELP, and each called a Hazard Prevention Advocate (HPA) who would be selected at each plant with unions choosing one-half of these positions. A minimum of two HPAs would be required at each plant with their total number based on the size of the company. There could be as many as 14 HPAs at companies with 500 or more employees. The HPAs would be permitted up to 16 hours off from work per month (22 hours for companies with 500 or more employees)—with full pay—to perform their duties. In addition, they would also receive special training at business expense and have access to the entire facility.

Perhaps the most onerous aspect of HELP is its intrusion into a company's daily business operations. If an employee involved in hazard identification, reduction, or prevention was dismissed or transferred, the HPA must be notified and afforded the opportunity to participate in the hiring of any new employee for that position, including the right to receive an applicant's résumé and to question the prospective employee.

Further, the company must justify in writing its reasons for changing chemicals, equipment, processes, even vendors and subcontractors, or when a plant would be expanded or closed! The notice would include an evaluation of the anticipated results from the change, any alternatives considered, and reasons why the alternative was accepted or rejected.

If an HPA believes in "good faith" that an imminent hazard exists, he can require the manager to shut down the entire facility, and there is nothing that can be done until a government representative is available to investigate the complaint. Should an unusual spill, leak, emission, etc., occur at the plant, the company would be required to notify each group, in writing, of the situation. Federal and state agencies would also require notification. After such an occurrence, the company would be subject to monthly inspections by the different groups for up to six months.

Obviously, the potential for abusing this law, particularly during labor contract negotiations, is great. Yet the penalties for employees as proposed, are relatively minor. For a single "unreasonable" abuse, an employee could be suspended for five days without pay. A second abuse in two years would result in a thirty day suspension without pay. Only after three "unreasonable" abuses within three years could an employee be terminated.

However, employers face fines up to $10,000 a day and more if they violate any portion of this act including punitive damages and court costs. Moreover, the businessman is presumed guilty if evidence merely "tends" to show guilt, and he can only hurdle such presumption with "clear and convincing" evidence. While no one wants hazardous conditions to exist, we should not allow vigilantism to be condoned under the guise of environmental protection.

Under the cloak of environmentalism, activists may run other peoples businesses *without investing one dollar, possessing any expertise, or exhibiting professionalism.* It is an environmental Trojan Horse.

In May 1991, the Hazard Elimination through Local Participation Act (HELP) was approved by the New Jersey Assembly Energy and Environment Committee after having undergone some additional minor changes. However, the HELP Act remained an excessively burdensome bill that would saddle business with expensive new requirements, inspections, and regulations.

Despite the changes, the bill is fundamentally and conceptually un-American and will serve only to discourage new investment and development. At a time when the state is in need of new economic growth, a law that would impose requirements stricter than anywhere else in the country will be a disincentive for business expansion. The new provisions, although slightly different from its inception, are as follows:

–It would create and empower Hazard Prevention Committees (HPCs) to inspect a facility without cause and for any reason!

–Consisting of equal numbers of management and union appointed "volunteers," HPCs would also be required at nonunion facilities and could serve as a tool for organizing.

–HPCs could be used for harassment rather than as a means of ensuring workplace safety.

–Local Emergency Planning Committees (LEPCs), created under the federal right-to-know law, would be given broad new powers not limited to their original intent of emergency response planning. Comprising both government officials and community representatives, LEPCs would have the right to inspect a facility for virtually any reason because of the broad definition of the term "hazard" in the bill.

–LEPCs would be required to inspect the entire facility every year. Such inspections, without cause, reason, or justification are excessive and bear no relationship to workplace safety. As a result, they may lead to instances of harassment, particularly during periods of labor-management negotiations.

Businesses operating in this modern world are already inspected numerous times a year by a myriad of government bureaus at the federal, state, county, and local levels and by a number of agencies, including various worker health (OSHA) and safety bureaus. The HELP Act tells business that none of the existing government agencies can be trusted. It does this while unfairly and wrongly raising concern for health and safety in the community. There is no estimate or consideration given in the bill to the economic cost to both business and the government for implementation of its provisions.

Hence, another "Son of ECRA" may yet be born. It has not yet been enacted as this book goes to press. One can legitimately ask: How could something like this be proposed in a democratic society? It's easy to answer that question. Few legislators have the fortitude to confront the grassroots environmentalist movement as it now exists. The business community that provides the taxes, jobs, and economic growth is depicted as the "bad guys." The people in the green hats are perceived as the "good guys." Opposition is painted as anti-environment or as polluters attempting to avoid penalties.

The environmental movement has done a fantastic "PR Job" on all of us, while opponents of HELP have said:

> Every paragraph spells paperwork, bureaucracy and added costs—both for the state and private sector," complained Assemblyman Arthur Albohn (R-Morris), the only member of the committee to vote against the bill (A.2832). "It's a gross intrusion into the private sector."
>
> James Morford, of the New Jersey State Chamber of Commerce, said the bill "would cast in concrete New Jersey's reputation as being the most blatantly hostile state in the nation for most manufacturing enterprises."
>
> Other business lobbyists expressed doubts over whether the bill would withstand a court challenge, saying it suffers from legal flaws because of intrusions into labor law and federal Occupational Safety and Health Administration standards.[9]

It would be a mistake to believe that this type of thinking is a New Jersey or localized phenomenon. Under the cloak of hazardous materials, safety, or dangerous environmental conditions, laws can be proposed without traditional regard to citizens' rights. This kind of thinking was the basis for advocacy of New Jersey "HELP." Unfortunately, this cloak is also being used nationally. As reported by the Commerce and Industry Association in February of 1992, a federal clone has been introduced.

NATIONAL "HELP" ACT PROPOSED

Using many of the same flawed arguments which proponents of the New Jersey HELP Act used while promoting their massive intrusion into labor management relation issues, United States Senators Ford, Kennedy and Metzenbaum have introduced legislation that would attempt to achieve many of the same results. The Bill numbers are H.R.3160: Representative Ford (D-MI); S.1622: Senator Kennedy (D-MA), Senator Metzenbaum (D-OH).

The legislation, titled "The Comprehensive Occupational Safety and Health Reform Act," is really the New Jersey HELP Act on a federal level. It would require companies with eleven or more employees to set up health and safety committees comprising equal numbers of labor and management representatives and would permit employees to shut any company down!

Employers would be required to implement a written safety and health program detailing methods and procedures for identifying, evaluating, documenting, correcting, and investigating occupational accidents, illnesses and fatalities at each work site. Training courses would be mandated at employer expense; employees would be permitted to challenge as inadequate any citations and fines levied by OSHA; and they could refuse to work if they have "reasonable apprehension" that their duties would result in serious injury. Any employee claiming such apprehension would have to be paid. Penalties under this bill could go as high as $250,000 for individuals, $500,000 for corporations and would include jail time as long as ten years for a first offense and twenty years for subsequent offenses!

This national "HELP" Act would impose vast new paperwork burdens on employers, particularly small businesses and would give workers substantial authority, but no accountability in major management areas.[10]

While the federal "HELP" legislation is being debated, New Jersey has installed another onerous first. In response to the mass hysteria sweeping New Jersey, a new post has been created—that of environmental prosecutor. One of the first actions of the new prosecutor was to involve all citizens.

As I have said earlier, the public is being urged to report pollution by calling 1-800-NJ-CLEAN. The environmental prosecutor's office is soliciting citizen tips on polluters. In one of his first pronouncements, he has called upon boaters, beachcombers, fishermen, hunters, and factory workers to form a network of "observers" and report other citizens to authorities. Forget that these citizens may not know what they are observing or have other axes to grind.

Imagine unskilled, undeputized citizens being urged to turn in their neighbors for environmental crimes. In New Jersey it can be done with a certain aplomb since state officials not only are suggesting it but are setting it up.

Citizens can report drums of water, emissions of steam, and the loading and unloading of trucks while perched on hillsides with binoculars. Those who are licensed pilots can circle local factories or facilities seeking violators. Quiet balloonists can sneak up close to photograph transgressors. Unfortunately, the idea is not a joke but another proud New Jersey first.

> New Jersey's, and the nation's first environmental prosecutor warned polluters yesterday that the state is turning to the public to report pollution activities by simply calling 1-800-NJ-CLEAN.
>
> That's the new hot line number that Steven J. Madonna intends to install to allow anyone to tip off authorities on pollution incidents the moment they occur anywhere in the state.
>
> He announced the new number at yesterday's fifth annual conference of the New Jersey Environmental Federation, attended by some 400 people at the Berkeley Carteret Hotel in Asbury Park.
>
> Madonna who did not say when the new number will be ready for use, called on New Jersey's grass roots activists to be the quiet observers of the environmental scene.
>
> The public network, he said, will be backed up by some 7,000 government employees in the Marine Police, State Police, Attorney General's Office, the Department of Environmental Protection and Energy (DEPE) and other agencies, all of whom will be ready to follow through at the administrative, civil and criminal levels to apprehend and prosecute the polluter.[11]

Unfortunately, a government that can't retain its balance during a period of hysteria will lose its footing also. Alexander Hamilton warned George Washington that "the people could not be trusted to retain democracy." Hamilton was correct; 1-800-NJ-CLEAN proves it!

Measures like these have brought us closer and closer to George Orwell's vision in "1984." While there certainly is no freedom to pollute, we must be wary of giving up hundreds of years of hard-earned rights to those who wish to take these freedoms away for environmental or any other reasons.

In addition to deputizing citizens, New Jersey is now preparing to finance a hunt for random targets.

Environmental "Vigilante" Fund Proposed

The New Jersey State Chamber of Commerce had spoken out in opposition to *legislation that would allow self-appointed environmental and public interest organizations to contest the issuance of DEPE permits,* bringing the permit process to a virtual standstill. The bill (S-3035) would also *establish the Environmental Litigation Defense Fund* with a start-up appropriation of $1 million and additional monies to be derived from penalties paid under the Water Pollution Control Act. *The funds would be doled out by the Public Advocate to "public interest groups" to attack business.*[12]

If this bill becomes law, the state would take on a new role of funding attacks on citizens and businessmen, another encouragement to move elsewhere. Neither a healthy society nor a clean environment can be achieved by spying on one's neighbors. Indeed, the pendulum has, once again, swung too far.

What is the economic result of this bureaucratic overkill? On April 12,1990, a discussion was held in Plainfield, New Jersey, and chaired by Assemblyman Robert Franks, (R-Union). Its focus was to obtain ideas that would help to stem the economic losses caused by numerous regulatory issues including ECRA.

The conclusion was not promising. Franks said after the two hour meeting, that New Jersey's manufacturing industry is

> hemorrhaging, and communication between business and government on issues contributing to the problem could be the vital link in reversing the trend. . . . Over the last decade, New Jersey has lost 200,000 bluecollar jobs, 1,000 manufacturing plants and is left with about 600,000 manufacturing positions, its lowest level since 1939. We have to stop the hemorrhage and losses of a sector which for years has been the backbone of the state's economy.[13]

One of the attendees, businessman Edgar Otto, put it in very clear terms, "New Jersey doesn't want me . . . you're running me out of the state and the 300 jobs I've created." Otto has since decided that he would move to Arkansas, since his company competes globally. He and others mentioned six negatives of doing business in New Jersey at the meeting. There were (1) high health care and utility costs; (2) high income and property taxes; (3) high wages; (4) lack of affordable housing; (5) DEPE regulations, (6) ECRA.[14]

An economist, Laurence T. Clark, Jr., stated in the *Business Journal* of New Jersey that,

> the state does not have either the energy or regulatory climate to compete with other states. Its current regulatory scene and recent tax rate increases make the state uncompetitive with many others throughout the country. In [the] short run, the rapid rise in energy prices will transfer income to the energy-

exporting states from New Jersey. The result will be a lower standard of living for New Jerseyans and a lower rate of economic growth.[15]

We Must Bring the Pendulum Back to the Middle!

What can we do about environmental hysteria that has resulted in a combative regulatory framework and has led to a loss of jobs, a curtailment of freedoms, and economic stagnation. Sadly, the state's approach to the problem, as shown in these examples, will not improve the environment since environmental betterment can only be achieved by a joint cooperative effort at all levels. Improvement must utilize a rational partnership between the legislature, the regulators, the public, labor, and business.

We must all work together to calm the current hysteria, seek legislative changes, and restore an equitable regulatory climate. We can do that and also have a clean state and country in which to live. It takes calm leadership and cooperation—but it can be done! The pendulum must once again return to the middle.

V

Freedom of Speech—
Involuntary Servitude

"Congress shall make no law respecting an establishment of religion . . . or abridging the freedom of speech . . ."

"Neither slavery nor involuntary servitude except as a punishment for crime . . . shall exist within the United States . . ."

The above quotes are directly from the United States Constitution, Amendment I and XIII respectively. In New Jersey both of these hard-fought freedoms have been affected by environmental regulations. Unfortunately, there have been few protests.

There is no argument about the power of the NJDEPE to assess huge fines for minor infractions whether in ECRA or other related enforcement modes. These enormous fines have the power to still any protest. A citizen's assets can literally be taken without having been guilty of a major infraction.

Recall the story of Cleaveland Industrial Park. One of the owners contacted me and was so furious that he wanted to tell his side of the story. While the partnership was being fined $3,000,000 for problems they felt they didn't cause, noncompliance with that fine was threatened at treble damages.

Total destruction of their business and assets was threatened, and their personal lives were traumatized. They wanted to speak out but couldn't. Yet, they had been convicted of nothing except property ownership. It was their contention *that they had not caused any environmental harm.* But under the cloak of an environmental threat, they were battered into submission and couldn't speak out! Excessive fines can still any voice, as easily as a loaded "45."

Many people are unaware that the huge, burdensome ECRA fees and the NJDEPE fines are retained by or credited to that agency. In essence, their powers allow them to force self-incriminating filings, force compliance by fine, try your case in their system (the next appeal is usually the boss of the bureaucrat you dealt with), fine you and keep a portion of the collected monies.

Numerous New Jersey businessmen have stated their objections to this dictatorial system, but few have had the courage to confront such a powerful system. An exception has been the Commerce and Industry Association that has stood tall, even when losing the majority of the battles.

We offer two comments on the subject by two New Jersey businessmen who asked to remain anonymous:

1. It is obvious that a law whose implementation and interpretation is carried out by people whose salary depends on the law being widely interpreted and strongly implemented

does not belong in a democracy—no matter how well-intended the law was in its original form.

2. No, I am unable to assist your efforts; I'm fearful discussion could make compliance or resolve more restrictive. They have already used this tactic successfully on my company.[1]

One of the most successful tactics used by the NJDEPE to subtly curtail first amendment rights is their in-house referral system. If asked, they will deny its existence, but former officials have confided in me that it does indeed exist. I also personally have seen it in operation. The NJDEPE is comprised of numerous sub-organizations or fiefdoms that operate as if they were separate and independent.

A company was told to monitor a certain river for pollutants. The river ran along its property. This request was made to the management of that company while it was in an ECRA case, a very vulnerable period. The company's premises were adjacent to hundreds of feet of riverbank, but there were no drains, no run-off, and the company's operations had no apparent effect on the purity of the river water.

Realizing the magnitude of the request, the president refused. The ECRA agent told him that he had better rethink his position, or else. Soon, the company found out what the "or else" meant. Inspectors from four different departments descended on the property, checking hazardous wastes, sound decibels, trucking manifests, record keeping, etc. Somehow, the county health officer also showed up the following week. Since he was an honorable gentleman and knew what was happening, he looked the other way and said so. "I don't like these kinds of things," he stated. Two small fines resulted. A warning shot? Perhaps.

The president of the above company was indeed reminded who's the boss. A minor infraction fine of around $7,500 was assessed (amount changed to protect identity). When he called Trenton to appeal the fine, he was told by the appellate person (he's the fine issuer's boss), "There's no reason to come down here to appeal. Your fine *will not* be reduced, this was a warning." The World War II combat veteran caved in and said to this writer, "They have me, they can fine me out of business and take away my life's work. I have to shut up and just get through; please don't use my name."

ECRA is an involuntary filing, caused in many cases by a collateral voluntary action (sale of a business). But once in the Star Chamber proceedings and due to the enormous power of your adversary, your life can be battered into a submissive state. Of course, if you speak up, you can also be labeled "anti-environment," which makes any protest wrong on the face of it.

In case you believe this "stilling of dissent" is overblown, review the following case that clearly shows how NJDEPE regulatory overkill works at its zenith:

North Warren Regional High School was fined $750,000 by the NJDEPE for violating water pollution discharge limits in 1988 and 1989. In addition they were accused of improper record keeping.

The school officials were shocked by the size and intensity of the fine and requested a hearing with an administrative law judge. The officials said that they did not have sufficient funds to pay the penalty.

Superintendent Edward Herbert said: The school spent $20,000 to $25,000 to replace malfunctioning equipment and hired a new plant operator more than a year ago to rectify problems. The 20-year old plant discharges 6,000 to 7,000 gallons of treated wastewater daily into the *Paulins Kill* (a waterway), far below the plant's 20,000-gallon a day capacity," he said.

"Since August of last year, our plant has worked excellently," Herbert said. School officials were "quite taken aback" by the size of the fine since they [believed] most of the violations [were] minor, he said.

Shapella [the DEPE official in charge of the investigation] said the DEPE assesses penalties by judging the conduct of the permit holder and the seriousness of the infractions. The school is not accused of intentionally causing the pollution, and most of the violations were minor or moderate.[2]

Of course, fining a school district $750,000 can only result in higher property taxes for the area's innocent home owners. But the power of this devastating attack simply stills all opposition. Would you speak up if your life or business career could be ruined by an agency with this power? The only alternative is for the victim to take the state agency to court, in which case the delays and costs could easily destroy the victim anyway. While the case is being adjudicated, the plaintiff could be descended upon by a half a dozen related, but ostensibly independent bureaus. However, that would be only "a coincidence!"

In a letter to *The Star Ledger,* published on October 18, 1988, a former New Jerseyan, Michael Kunz, put it this way:

The time has come for a criminal investigation of the New Jersey Department of Environmental Protection and Energy (DEPE) to begin. Under current policy, either written or assumed, the DEPE has become its own governing body, writing the laws at will with no legislative body to represent the public, enforcing these laws on a guilty-till-proven-innocent basis, and trying the accused in its own court system.

The time has long since passed that New Jersey's big industries should band together and form a coalition to fight the current unconstitutional actions of this Gestapo-like organization. There is no reason we can't have a clean and decent environment and a DEPE which falls under proper control by the people whom they were established to serve.

I moved out of New Jersey because government is out of control in the state. The DEPE is just another example of how right Edmund Burke was when he said, "The only thing necessary for the triumph of evil is for good men to do nothing."

The DEPE is the embodiment of the incompetent, led by the blind, claiming to help the unknowing, while creating a haven of employment for those who can't succeed in a real job. May God have mercy on New Jersey.

On September 10, 1990, the DEPE announced the fining of seven New Jersey businesses. These companies included: Sphinx Electroplating Corporation, Passaic Township, $967,500; Bates Manufacturing Company, Washington Township, $413,500; and Frank's Sanitation Service, Riverdale, $294,500.

Hassanein Soliman, vice president of Sphinx, questioned why his ten year old company was fined nearly one million dollars when its gross annual sales were only $200,000? "It's a telephone number fine," he quipped. "You get it out of the phone book."

Soliman said that the test samples used by the DEPE were inaccurate because the laboratory gave Sphinx contaminated bottles. The company has switched laboratories and always used a lab that was certified by the DEPE, contrary to the state's accusation, he said.

Soliman said the sampling was done when the plant was not operating, a cost-saving measure that was verbally approved by the DEPE. The company, which does military and industrial work, should not be fined and has requested a hearing, he said.

"We don't feel we were doing anything we weren't supposed to be doing," Soliman said. We are in this town not to pollute the river. We'd like to stay in this town."[3]

The issue above is not who is right or wrong. The real issue is what's going on? When a company does $200,000 in gross annual sales, and an agency fires off a $967,500 fine, they are simply aiming a missile at the business, its jobs, and the lives and assets of all those associated with their target. Could you fight back? Would you speak up? Or, caught like a rat in a trap, would you knuckle under and do what you are told? If so victimized a company can attempt to sue in court. However, few small companies have the wherewithal to beat a state or federal agency in court. This, while given as an alternative, is really not a practical alternative due to time and cost.

How does the stilling of dissent relate to "involuntary servitude?" In many cases ECRA is an incarceration-like sentence for those individuals caught in its web. During an ECRA filing period, which can last one to five years, the individual is mentally, financially, and philosophically in jail. The story of a European survivor of World War II will show this aspect.

An eighty-one year old gentleman called me about his problem and asked if I could help him. He owned a wholesale dry-cleaning business in Northern New Jersey and a 10,000 square foot building. He sold his business, not knowing about the wiles of ECRA, and was now caught in its web.

His lawyer (not an environmental attorney) had told him, "you just have to file a few papers, and it would only take ninety days." Once he was in ECRA's grasp, he realized that it would be more like hundreds of pages, two to three years in time, and possibly cost him $150,000. His business was located in an old building built in the 1890s, which he had owned for the past twenty years. He said he had never polluted anything, but, because of the building's obvious age he didn't know what he might find at the site. "The other owners and tenants are all gone or dead; I don't know what's there." Then he related his feelings:

> Mr. Siminoff, I am eighty-one years old and ill. I must retire. I only have two to three years to live at the most. I escaped the Nazis and came here, never heard of this ECRA, and can't imagine why my retirement money and assets are being taken from me when I didn't do anything or pollute the property. Is there anything I can do to get out of this, since I will be dead before it's finished? I don't want to dump the burden on my wife; she's seventy-eight.

This man's case has always stuck in my mind because it clearly shows what happens to an elderly businessman whose only crimes were property ownership and the attempt to retire. His obituary in the newspaper about a year after the telephone call clearly showed that this dry cleaner never made that retirement; he died while in ECRA. His wife probably did inherit the burden! What was her crime? It was being married to a man who had a business in an old building and who wanted to retire. But their retirement assets were taken from them without explanation or understanding.

This book is not a debate about cleaning up the environment. Cleaning up New Jersey or the United States is a valid objective. However, our constitutional protections and our Declaration of Independence were created because of harassment suffered by the authors of those documents. Our forefathers wanted future generations to be free of governmental harassment *even for good sounding causes*. They wanted to protect *bad* speech, *bad* religions, *bad* newspapers, and *plain old ornery people*. They wanted us to be free! The zeal of good causes didn't impress them as much as protecting our citizens against the "good causes." A good cause, "environmentalism," is no excuse to place free citizens in involuntary servitude, nor is it a reason to pauperize an innocent property owner.

The NJDEPE, however, does not recognize innocence as an excuse. Nor does the DEPE allow constitutional protections to get in the way of their mission or mandate to "clean up or else."

The following story was told by a New Jersey businessman caught squarely in ECRA's vise. It has been slightly edited because he does not wish his company to be identified.

Our company made an ECRA application, expecting to sell our business and/or property. Since the transaction was complicated, we believed that an ECRA clean-up would have to be performed only if the sale took place. The ECRA submittal application was approved under these conditions, but the DEPE issued an order dictating that clean-up be started at once, sale or no sale. Our caseworker simply gave us such a letter, and expected us to comply, forthwith.

Our business is located on a landfill over a large, previously polluted river. The fill material was dredged up over 100 years ago from the river's bottom. Our neighbor's property and much of our surrounding area was created in the same manner a long time ago. I believe that some of this was undertaken under the auspices of the United States Army Corps of Engineers, and they used the engineering technology (science) of the time.

Sometimes, at high tide, the river came up to ground-floor level, so that, in our case, a clean-up could conceivably include cleaning up the river.

Our company, despite the river under us, has been operating at its present site many years without a recorded spill or pollution incident.

In order to get into the ECRA system, we had to pay approximately $10,000 in filing fees immediately, and initiate a letter of credit at our bank in a huge amount (issued in favor the NJDEPE) costing our company another $10,000 fee. The letter of credit was backed by a bond and a pledge of assets of the several partners. Unless we knuckled under to their order, DEPE threatened to move in on us, at great cost and expense, with their enforcement battalions, which could totally disrupt our operations. This action would, most probably, put us out of business before we had a chance to sell our property.

Due to a change in market conditions and the realities of cleaning up the river, no sale of our property is possible nor, practically speaking, ever in sight. The real estate "wetlands" market is dead as a doornail. The caseworker who wrote us that the clean-up was necessary is no longer pressing the case because he left the department. The new caseworker is taking a different tack. We believe our ECRA case is now on "hold." If a sale were to be consummated sometime in the future, we would have to once again enter the costly ECRA process and probably never would make it through the system.

I certainly am not opposed to a cleaner environment, nor to working in good faith and within reason toward that end. Still, as the lady on the Titanic said: "I rang for ice, but this is ridiculous!"[4]

The ECRA process, when combined with federal wetlands regulations and other overzealous enforcement, can destroy the property rights of any citizen who owns real estate near fresh or salt water. At a meeting of the "Raritan Bay Property Owners Association," it was stated by their attorney that these owners are firmly stuck in a pile of nearly-dry cement. They can't clean up their property because it is repolluted by the tides. They can't sell the property, can't change its use (that could trigger ECRA), can't lease it (landlord and renter can be jointly and severally liable), and can't remortgage it (the bank has secondary liability). In essence regulations prohibit the use and enjoyment of their own property.

Yet these property owners must pay real estate taxes, insurance, and all other costs related to property ownership. This same "illegal taking" is forced upon owners of wet property, old buildings, or a variety of other sites.

Decades of old pollution occurring in urban areas offer owners of old buildings no choice but to abandon their property. In some cases these owners are forced to leave their property and flee the jurisdiction because they are fearful of "opening Pandora's box," hence being wiped out financially. In the continuation of the ECRA nightmare, this abandonment then passes the properties on to the cities, who seize them for nonpayment of real estate taxes. When faced with ownership of a now worthless piece of property, what can the city do? If the costs of clean-up are more than the property is worth many people stop paying their taxes and/or leave it to the city. Property is being abandoned rather than cleaned up because the NJDEPE can make an individual, the owner, personally liable for clean-up—even if the pollution is not of his or her doing. Once named the PRP (Principal Responsible Person) an individual is hooked, personally, even if totally innocent!

The PRP is in a catch-22. Clean up the mess you didn't make with your time and money; fill out the forms under penalty of perjury; self-incriminate yourself and your business by doing so; and finish this job or you may even go to jail. If you start a clean-up and leave hazardous materials on your premises for too long a time, you can be cited criminally. Recall the Irvington, New Jersey, case. The same thing can occur in federal jurisdiction.

It is necessary to interject a collateral thought at this juncture. Up to this point we have talked about the power of making regulations, issuing fines, and controlling the appellate process, etc. But now think about the ultimate power.

The NJDEPE not only can make the rules of the game, it can select the substances it doesn't like. In New Jersey the DEPE has promulgated regulations about leaves (the kind that drop from trees), grass clippings, and boy scout and high school bonfires (they are prohibited). One of the most far-reaching moves was to include "oil" as a hazardous waste. Once oil was included, which everyone has or uses, unbelievable snares, traps, paperwork requirements, manifests, etc., can be set up.

If you file under ECRA and have drums of oil, such as in a machine shop, the oil has *to be handled as a hazardous waste*. Hazardous wastes have their own sets of collateral rules. Keeping hazardous wastes on a property in violation of those rules (even though you don't pollute) can subject one to criminal penalties. Hence, the cross-hatching of environmental regulation can still the most courageous voice. No one wants to go to jail.

Most court cases heard to date have been decided in favor of the state agencies. The most important recent case was decided on May 6, 1991 (See Appendix 1). This case was brought by various industry and public interest groups against certain NJDEPE regulations. In most aspects of the case the court held for the regulators. In two areas, however, the court changed direction.

> With regard to the appellants' challenge of the NJDEPE's regulation requiring ECRA compliance in the case of partial condemnations of industrial establishments, the Court held that the NJDEPE's regulation applying ECRA to condemnations, partial or otherwise, is eminently reasonable and sustainable. The Court noted that the Act applies to a change in ownership *(N.J.S.A. 13:1k-8(b))* and condemnation does result in a change in ownership. It also reasoned that the concern that hazardous substances be cleaned up when an industrial establishment ceases operations is perhaps more compelling when the transferee is a public body than when an industrial establishment is transferred to a private entity, since the public entity may have lesser resources with which to correct environmental problems. The Court concluded that it would be inequitable to permit a landowner to avoid ECRA compliance by the "fortuitous event" of partial or complete condemnation.
>
> As to the appellants' contention that it is unreasonable and beyond the scope of the ECRA statute to require compliance when there is only a partial condemnation and an industrial establishment continues to operate on the site, the Court

stated that the NJDEPE's decision to require review of an entire site, when real property comprising more than 20 percent of the total value of the industrial property is conveyed, is in accord with the purpose of ECRA and is a reasonable exercise of the NJDEPE's discretion in implementing broad statutory language.

The Court also acknowledged that the problem of partial conveyances had been addressed by the NJDEPE in order to further the legislative purpose of preventing the abandonment of industrial sites.

The appellants argued that the applicability provisions of the ECRA regulations, particularly those concerning parent-subsidiary issues, violated the Commerce Clause of the United States Constitution (the "clause"). Appellants contended that the applicability provisions of the ECRA regulations directly and significantly burden interstate and international commerce. The appellants offered, by way of example of alleged impermissible burdens placed on interstate commerce, various corporate transactions in which a corporation in another state (or country) has a subsidiary or operation in New Jersey which functions as an "industrial establishment." More specifically, they reasoned that the NJDEPE's ability to void a transaction for failure to comply with ECRA, unconstitutionally burdens interstate commerce. The Court held that although the NJDEPE has the power to void such out-of-state/country transactions for failure to comply with the ECRA statute, the regulation does not unconstitutionally burden interstate (or international) commerce. The Court explained that while a state law that is motivated by economic protectionism and which directly and intentionally burdens interstate commerce will almost certainly be held invalid, much more latitude is afforded state law which advances legitimate state interests. The Court concluded that ECRA furthers a legitimate local interest. It found that environmental and public health concerns, when not expressly preempted by federal law, are legitimate and compelling state concerns. The Court rejected the notion that ECRA impedes the flow of out-of-state commerce into the state and that it directly or sweepingly burdens interstate transactions. Finally, the Court found that there is no conflict with, or preemption by, federal statutes or environmental regulations.[5]

The court decision succeeded in increasing the pain of ECRA. If a government agency were to take a part of your land for a road, park, or other public use, this could become an ECRA-triggering event. A small seizure of land can force ECRA onto an unsuspecting owner, and force him to enter clean-up proceedings on the entire site. This was found to be a reasonable exercise of the broad statutory language. Unfortunately, the constitutionality of ECRA was ducked. While there was only a narrow challenge under the "Commerce Clause," the court saw no impediment to this aspect.

The court came down strongly on the side of the lawmakers and regulators without regard to protection of the individual citizen. If one reads the entire decision, it becomes immediately apparent that individual rights will not be protected by the New Jersey legislature, the NJDEPE, or the Appellate Section of the Superior Court system when stacked up against the environment. While this may come as no surprise, it nevertheless was a totally disappointing turn of events.

Since New Jerseyans have been cowed into submission and have chosen not to fight back to regain their legal rights, some of them have just left the state and abandoned properties and buildings that reverted to the cities. Upon taking the property for tax lien, the cities get ECRA because they now become the current owners. In 1990 Trenton, New Jersey, had fourteen buildings in this category. These buildings were abandoned for a variety of reasons, some because the clean-up standards could not be achieved. The city (now the owner) could not meet the standards either. The results were lost jobs, abandoned properties, lives destroyed, the economy damaged, and civil rights obliterated.

As Mayor Carmen J. Armenti, of Trenton, New Jersey, said in a letter to this author in January 1990:

> The ECRA problem has become especially acute in urban areas where private firms either do not have or are not inclined to invest the resources necessary for the clean-up of industrial buildings and sites. New Jersey cities are more and more faced with a scenario of owners abandoning industrial properties and stopping further tax payments. These properties are then effectively removed from the city's ratable base. Jobs are lost and future development is stymied because of the prohibitive costs of environmental clean-up.
>
> The cities do not have the financial resources to deal with the problem.

These tentacles of state environmental agencies can snag anyone. A trustee of an estate can be named a PRP—so can a widow. In a Union County New Jersey case, an estate was drained by the ECRA filing. The executor was brought into it and had to provide his own funds (and his time) for a case that had no business relationship to him.

Banks, insurance companies, and mortgage holders who take over defaulted property are the new "current owners." They must take the property through the ECRA Star Chamber process.

Suppose you lend money to a company with the loan secured by a property. The company fails and you take the property back. The cost of clean-up can exceed your loan, but as the new owner, you must clean it up under ECRA. You didn't dirty the property—you just made a business loan. Yet *your property* (the loan proceeds) is taken from you and given to the state "without regard to fault." You did nothing except make a loan.

Another anonymous businessman put it this way:

> ECRA is the most onerous law New Jersey has ever put into effect. Small privately held companies are held hostage to its requirements. We have sold our company and needed to comply. The process was time consuming, overregulated, not responsive and downright extortive! I would NEVER consider putting an industrial facility in New Jersey again. Too costly and risky. Our *ACO* (Administrative Consent Order) was received, but after sixteen months we still have not resolved mitigation [agreed clean-up] procedures.[6]

The businessman's word was extortion, and its linkage was correct!

During the summer of 1991, the mayor of a small town in northeast New Jersey filed a site plan to develop his property. The property encompassed fifteen acres and bordered Route 206. The site plan was approved by the planning board of Montague. The engineers who counseled the property owner during the approval process had foreseen no major obstacles.

In order to develop the site, the owner, Joseph Barbagallo, cut down thirty to forty trees to pave the way for his project. The trees were cut after the receipt of site plan approval by the town.

While the property owner believed that receipt of a site plan approval was sufficient—it wasn't. The NJDEPE got into the act, stating that the thirty to forty trees were cut on the property without receiving a "Freshwater Wetlands Protection Act" permit. The permit was supposedly required even though the trees were not located on wetlands. It was alleged that part of the property was located on wetlands, but that section of the property was undisturbed by the owner's actions. The owner felt that site plan approval was all that was required to cut down the trees.

The NJDEPE would not back down from its position and fined the owner $10,000 per day for thirty-six days. The total fine was $360,000. This fine was issued for cutting down trees *on one's own property.*

The owner did not have the money to pay the fine or fight the agency. His feelings about the matter are quite clear:

"It shows how ruthless the government can be," he said. "I offered to restore the land, plant trees and do anything to make it environmentally better, even though we followed the letter of the law. That was not good enough"

[The owner] said the property was "manipulated out from under" him by the DEPE.

"They levy unbelievable fines . . . bring you to your knees, then demand you continue paying the taxes and clean up the land of debris from bygone decades when the entire parcel was developed. Then they will take it from you in lieu of the fine."

The mayor insisted he is the victim of government strong-arm tactics.

. . . if we allow continuance of this type of control over our lives and properties we have carved still another notch, among the many the government has already accumulated, in taking our freedoms and rights."

[The owner] contends it is unfair for the state to concoct laws prohibiting development of wetlands without compensating the landowners for loss of their investments.

"If privately owned land is truly environmentally sensitive, it should be purchased by all the taxpayers because it is all taxpayers that benefit," [the owner] reasoned. "People should not be compelled to fund a system that treats citizens as though they were the enemy."[7]

What was the settlement penalty for cutting down trees on one's own property after receipt of site plan approval? The state took the owner's land. In turn, the state is offering the land for one dollar to the "Natural Lands Trust." The land will be preserved as open space forever.

While the above case was not within the purviews of ECRA, it clearly shows the ECRA thought process. Environmental good is superior to an owner's rights or constitutional guarantees of fairness and due process. The government justifies environmental bullying. A citizen land owner has no protection when accused of environmental transgressions, even if the accusations are slender or ridiculous.

Paradoxically, ECRA can be deemed New Jersey's "legalized bank-robbing law" because of a case in which a businessman had his credit cut off by a bank because he had been involved in an ECRA case. He deftly succeeded in having his credit reinstated by threatening to declare total bankruptcy, thereby sticking the bank with the clean-up cost as the new owner. The extortion process was just passed down the line from the state, to the business, and to the bank.

VI

The Anatomy of ECRA

Simply stated, the practical scope of ECRA and its effect on the life of an applicant is "mind-boggling."

Most people fall into the ECRA trap inadvertently. Until one is in the game, most businessmen cannot believe the cost, intensity, depth, and pervasiveness that influences their lives while in the ECRA process.

Two businessmen made anonymous comments that are pertinent to the despair one feels in ECRA. The first wrote:

> We own two multi-leased factory buildings in Essex County and have under twenty tenants. We have been unable to remortgage, unable to finance, and (of course) can't sell them. They are older type buildings and have about ten ECRA subject tenants. [The remaining tenants are exempt from ECRA; one is a shoe store.] We are absolutely stuck and can't figure any way out. After twenty years of paying down

the mortgage, I am afraid to reinvest my own funds. I guess that after my death they will become in disuse—it's a strange way to reward me (I didn't pollute) for hard work; and a strange way to clean up New Jersey.

The second businessman observed:

We would be more than happy to discuss our nightmare with you. We have canceled plans to build another facility in New Jersey. Our company will be relocating to Pennsylvania due to ECRA. We are not in any way polluting the environment; however, the time and money required to comply with ECRA has made it impossible for our business to operate in New Jersey any longer.[1]

The above two comments represent the inner feelings of two small businessmen. This deep feeling is especially prevalent in those who did not pollute their property, nevertheless are "jointly and severally liable." Large companies, who can afford the cost of bureaucratic red tape, have found the ECRA concept equally bewildering, but manageable economically.

Why are there seemingly more problems in New Jersey? To go back in time, iron furnaces were first used in the 1740s, and from that time forward New Jersey has been known as an industrial state. Its proximity to major cities, transportation networks, and natural resources have historically made New Jersey a prime location for industry.

An unfortunate byproduct of New Jersey's industrial past is its environmental present. Since the industrial era preceded the era of responsible environmental management, New Jersey has the dubious distinction of being home to more "Superfund" waste sites than any other state. In an effort to protect the public interest in a clean environment as well as to improve the state's tarnished "chemical alley" image, New Jersey developed a host of aggressive and far-reaching environmental protection programs. To address the particularly distressing prospect of abandoned and/or contaminated industrial properties and to protect innocent purchasers, ECRA was passed into law in 1983, taking effect at the end of that year. The major thrust of ECRA required that industrial properties undergo state-supervised environmental audits and receive NJDEPE approval prior to sale or transfer. This was how ECRA began, but it has mushroomed to become far-reaching, omnipresent, and suffocating.

It must be clearly stated again, however, that New Jersey's industrial future is very much threatened by the unfair and overzealous administration of ECRA and related environmental legislation. Together they form a web of suffocating regulations under the guise of societal good.

Since enactment, ECRA has caused delays, excessive expense, confusion, and frustration for the business community. The NJDEPE has received continuous complaints and criticisms regarding ECRA, yet has rejected most suggestions for changes, apparently preferring the lengthiest, most pervasive regulations it can construe from the Act. In fact, in some ways the most recent revisions (as well as the appellate court decision; Appendix 1) to ECRA regulations have actually expanded the program well beyond the scope of the original law. Most businessmen have refrained from challenging these changes for fear that fighting back is viewed as "anti-environmental," and will cast them or their business in a bad public light.

The responsible agencies have extended their purview well beyond environmental concerns. The tone of the ECRA regulations and the history of its administration have enlarged the perception that New Jersey is hostile toward industry. While few companies will say it publicly, many refuse to locate any new industrial operations in New Jersey. In 1987, New Jersey lost 17,000 manufacturing jobs, despite a generally robust economy. From 1981 to 1991, nearly 1,000 plants have closed and more than 200,000 blue collar jobs have been lost. Many of these losses can be laid right at ECRA's doorstep.

Since excessive environmental regulation is generally aimed at manufacturing rather than shoe stores or ice cream parlors, it has some far-reaching effects. One of the least known but most easily understood is that these regulations harm minorities. Inner city manufacturing jobs have a higher percentage of minority workers than suburban factories. The simple reason is that more Blacks, Puerto Rican and other minority workers tend to live there. Inner cities have been the hardest hit by excessive environmental regulation.

Large companies will pay the required fees, go through the elongated process, and then simply expand elsewhere. They can usually afford to be burned once. Small and medium-sized businesses get caught and just cannot afford to pay the enormous costs that are required.

A technique used by many businesses to circumvent these unfair rules is to reduce their New Jersey exposure and plant size slowly, and to build up an equal facility elsewhere. In this way ECRA is never triggered. Officers of one large international company stated that it would cost more than 50 million dollars to ECRA their more than 100 acres. They explained that the property is not severely polluted, but they know it will not pass muster. Rather than spend this amount of money, they have adopted a five year plan. They are expecting to reduce the size of the employment at the facility each year by about 15 percent. At the fifth year they will have a smaller facility remaining with 25 percent of their starting employees. Most of their manufacturing operations will have been transferred to other states. The surrounding property will remain fallow, except for the small residual operations left there.

Many companies are adopting this "sneak out" approach to avoid bankruptcy. In many cases it's not that they do not wish to clean up, it's that they cannot afford to do so. Hence, survival is at stake. The result is New Jersey will lose manufacturing jobs steadily, its economy will weaken, and environmental clean-up will not occur. These types of job losses are especially severe in urban areas like Newark, Trenton, Passaic, and Patterson where old properties predominate.

Permanent job losses in the state and nation will likely continue until we change our approach toward environmental regulation from the present Draconian system to a system that's fair, consistent, and that creates minimal disruption to business operations and transactions.

The best solution for ECRA is to repeal the act and start over with new legislation! But since repeal may be unlikely, the following is a partial list of some of the most glaring defects in the current ECRA regulations together with some possible solutions.

Industrial Classifications

ECRA applicability is based in part upon property use. The current use of the Standard Industrial Classification (SIC) system for determining ECRA applicability is badly flawed and inconsistent. ECRA regulates such clean industries as sewing shops and basket weaving, yet exempts junk yards, chemical research testing laboratories, dry-cleaning plants, gasoline stations, and other businesses that handle significant quantities of hazardous substances. ECRA exempts auto and truck repair businesses, yet regulates motorcycle and forklift truck repair businesses. Warehousing of finished products is regulated by ECRA if conducted by a manufacturer, but usually not regulated if conducted by a wholesale distributor.

There are two potential solutions to the SIC problem. The first solution would be to conduct a careful, pragmatic review of the entire SIC manual and produce a logical, consistent list of environmentally suspect property uses that should remain subject to ECRA review. The second solution would be to eliminate the use of the SIC manual entirely and to base ECRA applicability upon the nature and quantity of hazardous substances used in the operations at the property in question. Perhaps the information submitted under the "Right-to-Know" program could be utilized for determining ECRA applicability, thereby connecting both programs.

Use of Hazardous Substances

Besides having a regulated SIC number, hazardous substances must be used or stored in order for the property to be considered an "industrial establishment" subject to ECRA. There are two problems with this criterion. First, it does not consider how the hazardous substances are used. Heating fuels and building maintenance products, such as paints and cleansers, should not be used for determining one's ECRA applicability. These substances are found at virtually every property in the country, regardless of use. They pose no more of a threat to the environment at an industrial property than at a residential or commercial property. The distinguishing feature for ECRA applicability should be that significant quantities of hazardous substances are used, or wastes produced, in the actual operations of the business described by the SIC number. To look beyond these operations unfairly and irrationally makes no regulatory sense and results in the overregulation of many small and clean businesses.

Applicability

Another problem with the hazardous substance criterion is the way it is applied. For ECRA applicability, a dilute solution is given the same treatment as a pure hazardous solvent. The relative hazard of a mixture should be determined in the same way as the relative hazard of a waste—by toxicity, ignitability, reactivity, or corrosivity. The presence of a dilute floor-cleaning solution should not be considered of sufficient environmental concern to render that property subject to ECRA. The list of hazardous substances under ECRA is far too broad. Small quantities of paint, solvents, or cleaning solution should not be relevant to this type of regulation. As previously stated, New Jersey has made oil a hazardous substance. Should oil be treated the same as dangerous chemicals?

The Scope of the Regulations

The scope of transactions that trigger ECRA compliance is far too complex and far too broad. In simple terms ECRA was intended to regulate *the sale or closing of industrial*

establishments. The current treatment of the following transactions goes far beyond the original scope and intent of
ECRA.

Some of the nonbuy and sell events that can trigger ECRA
are:

- Death
- Bankruptcy
- Sales of common stock (on public stock exchange)
- Going public (change in ownership, control)
- Selling adjoining pieces of property, even if the property
  is virgin land
- A general partnership that manages a real estate project
  where a minority partner sells his interest
- Sales of subsidiaries (including L.B.O.'s back to the
  original management)
- Mergers
- Takeovers
- Partial or total condemnation by a city, state, or govern-
  mental authority. (Even a road widening could trigger
  ECRA.)

There are so many real and potential ECRA triggers that
they are now ingrained deeply into day-to-day management
decision making. The "applicability triggers" now cover a
multitude of ordinary business events.

If a company sells more than 50 percent of its cash assets
or investments, it could trigger ECRA; or, if a control person
of a public company, say the 55 percent owner, sells 6
percent (changing control), ECRA can be triggered to the
distress of the shareholders. ECRA can halt business moves
that have no environmental concerns at all. The best example

of this is when a small company might have to tie up a significant amount of its credit line with a bank in order to post financial security for an ECRA Administrative Consent Order (ACO) or clean-up plan approval. Its operations and financial capabilities may therefore be severely hindered until the process ends and its credit availability restored, often a wait of one to three years.

Underground Storage

The Underground Storage of Hazardous Substances Act was enacted on September 3, 1986. The Act states, "It is the intent of the legislature that the program established by this Act constitute the only program regulating underground storage tanks in this state." The NJDEPE program established to implement this Act was designed to regulate tanks in a fair, orderly manner on an ongoing basis. It is nearly impossible to do this in the middle of a business or real estate transaction. The NJDEPE *should abide by the stated intent* of the legislature *and not regulate underground storage tanks* under ECRA. But it does nevertheless. In today's industrial and commercial real estate market, tanks are typically tested prior to the sale of property whether ECRA applies or not. The effect of eliminating tanks from ECRA applicability consideration would be a substantial reduction in the number of ECRA applications received by NJDEPE and a more consistent, less discriminatory approach to underground tank regulation in New Jersey. Tanks should be regulated on an ongoing basis, which was the intent of the legislature. They should be eliminated from the ECRA process just like an elevator would be if you had an appropriate inspection certificate and permit.

DeMinimus Quantity Exemption

In the revised ECRA regulations, the NJDEPE provided a small quantity hazardous substance exemption, called the DeMinimus Quantity Exemption. It was provided in recognition of the many small, clean businesses that were being unnecessarily forced through the ECRA process. But the criteria to qualify for the DeMinimus Quantity Exemption are too narrow and are not consistent with the manner in which NJDEPE determines ECRA applicability. For applicability purposes, the applicant must describe the history of ownership and property use since December 31, 1983. Few properties meet the DEPE test of: "Sole and original owner or operator of the industrial establishment from the date of construction of the facility on the property." Many former manufacturing facilities were converted to warehouse or office uses prior to 1983 and hence may not be regulated by ECRA when sold today. The DeMinimus Quantity Exemption must be administered in a realistic, fair manner particularly in the older industrial cities. The present exemption provides little or no relief. The exemption should be available to anyone who owns property or a business whether or not he or she is the "sole and original owner." For environmental responsibility, what difference does it make if he or she is the third owner? But, unless one meets this very narrow criterion, he is thrown into the process, perhaps because of a few gallons of oil, paint, or solvents. Furthermore, the threshold quantities of hazardous substances in the present criteria are too low; many single family residences would not qualify due to storage of heating oil, paints, gasoline, cleansers, etc. Luckily, homes are not subject to ECRA, yet.

Completing the Forms

There is a multitude of common problems encountered by applicants in completing the ECRA forms (Appendix 3). This is because it is ex post facto (after the fact) regulation and requires information that current owners (especially of older properties) may not be able to produce. For example, on the site map the applicant must indicate paved vs. unpaved areas or the map is considered incomplete by the NJDEPE. Neither the regulations nor the instruction to the Site Evaluation Submission specifically identify the need for this type of information. Also, in the site-history section of the application, it is often difficult or impossible to account fully or accurately for all property uses since 1940. While property ownership records are available, property use records generally do not exist. The property may have changed use and/or ownership ten times in fifty-two years!

If an application is deemed incomplete, a minimum case processing delay of three to four weeks results—an extremely exasperating situation for an applicant making his best efforts to comply. This type of problem must be treated in a more rational manner in order to reduce the time and frustration associated with ECRA compliance.

Administrative Consent Order (A.C.O.)

In certain transactions, such as mergers, it is not possible or desirable to go through the normal ECRA process before closing a business deal. To address these situations, the NJDEPE has made a document available called an Administrative Consent Order (ACO). The ACO is essentially a contract wherein the regulated party agrees to post a financial assurance bond and agrees to pay higher penalties for non-compliance in exchange for being allowed to close a business arrangement. This avenue is open to larger, more powerful companies who can afford to post bonds or financial assurances. Most small companies cannot do this because it diminishes their credit line by an equal amount. The basic ECRA requirements remain essentially unchanged.

The ACO is not as beneficial to a business as it may first seem! The amount of financial assurance is established by NJDEPE and is generally much more than the actual cost for clean-up. (In the GE-RCA merger, the bond amount was $36 million.) The applicant must also waive certain legal rights in order to sell a property under an ACO. If he doesn't agree to these terms, he doesn't get the ACO. Few buyers are willing to close a transaction if there is a real possibility of contamination due to being liable "joint and severally." Fewer banks are willing to be lenders in a deal involving an ACO. They can also inherit liability. Practically speaking, the ACO is only available to applicants and buyers that have *very substantial financial resources*. The small businessman, or the small property owner, gets no relief from ACOs and is shut out of the process.

The ECRA Fee Schedule

Certain fees in the ECRA Fee Schedule are grossly unfair, arguably punitive, and should be drastically reduced or eliminated. For example, even though it is presently a standard requirement of the NJDEPE that underground tanks be tested, a sampling plan, which only proposes tank testing, is assessed a NJDEPE review fee of $3,000. Then, after the tank testing is completed, the applicant is assessed a sample data review fee of $1,000. The actual time and effort required to review the test proposal and the results are, in reality, minimal. This, like many other fees, are straight and simple extortion.

If you wish to find out if your company is subject to ECRA, include a $200.00 check for the yes or no. It's called an "applicability determination." If you don't send the money, they won't tell you whether the law applies.

Even in a moderate-sized case, the cost of filing fees alone can exceed $20,000. These fees only entitle you to file papers with the NJDEPE. You receive no other benefit. Suppose a man about to be shot by a firing squad was required to pay for his own bullet?

Recall the C & M case (a rather small one by ECRA standards). The owner, Cy Francus, stated:

> Our experience with E.C.R.A., however, has been a frustrating one. The paperwork is nightmarish, the rules and regulations can only be interpreted by the most astute attorneys, and the costs of dealing with E.C.R.A. can only be borne by companies with the assets of the Fortune 500.
>
> To give you some idea of what I mean, the cost to file the initial papers (Submission Report), with E.C.R.A. was $850 plus $6,000 in attorneys fees. The report was 145 pages in length. I cannot believe that anyone in E.C.R.A. read them all. Another report we were required to file, the Air Quality Report, was only 2 pages long, but cost an equally ridiculous $1,000. The worst part is that not a dime of the $7,850 we paid went toward cleaning up the environment, the purpose of the E.C.R.A. review.[2]

An anonymous manufacturer told us that he was in favor of ECRA, but ECRA within reason. This is the time for the government to listen to the people and form a Task Force of businessmen and legislators for ECRA reform. Who knows better than the people who have gone through ECRA. Areas that need to be reviewed are:

- Length of time to complete the ECRA process
- Costs
- Number of people needed to complete a clean-up—consultants, waste haulers, well drillers, excavators, geologists, engineers, lab services and professional cleaners
- Your own employees
- Better guidelines to follow for clean-up
- Better ECRA attitude by the state in working with corporations, keeping the above-mentioned in mind, to clean up the environment—not run people out of the state.

Fines

There are many fines specified in the ECRA regulations. Errors in paperwork and time delays by the filer can result in a hefty fine for violations where there is no willful intent or environmental damage. While NJDEPE is authorized to compromise and settle any claim, the settlements have usually been substantial. The applicant realistically has little power to fight NJDEPE on this issue.

There are several reasons why an applicant can only rarely challenge a fine successfully. First, they are costly to adjudicate. Second, the process of the fine appeal itself is lengthy and difficult. Third, ECRA is usually triggered when something else is going on, i.e., a sale, merger, acquisition, moving or expansion of the business, etc. Hence, one is typically in the middle of a business transaction that cannot be post-poned while litigating with the NJDEPE. Furthermore, in an ACO the NJDEPE requires the applicant to waive his rights as part of the contract. The fining power can be used as a heavy club to intimidate companies into submission. For this reason most companies will not speak about the NJDEPE's use of fines as a weapon. The agency can put a company out of business.

Strange Results

The ECRA fining power and its complexities produce strange twists:

- ECRA requires regulated parties to post financial assur-ances to guarantee compliance with approved clean-up plans and administrative consent orders. In 1990, ap-proximately $500 million in financial assurances were in the files of the ECRA program. It is believed that the NJDEPE has not at this writing called upon a posted financial assurance for ECRA compliance. To obtain a suitable financial assurance for ECRA, the applicant must pay a financial institution from one to three percent of its face value. In addition the assurances must be collateralized with other assets of the applicant or be taken from a business line of credit. The result is that applicants have paid millions of dollars to financial institutions to comply with ECRA, and they have been required to freeze $500 million of equity capital that could otherwise be used for financing their business, or for further economic development. This staggering amount comes entirely from the industrial sector of the state's economy, and the use of it has provided no tangible benefit to the state of New Jersey or its business community.

- For some properties where several ECRA-triggering events (such as sale of business followed by sale of property) have occurred, NJDEPE has required multiple applications, one for each transaction. This can be a paperwork nightmare as even the most simple application requires site maps, property history since 1940, a minimum of six notarized signatures to certifications and, of course, multiple fees.

- After completing the ECRA travail, the petitioner is granted sixty days to complete his business transaction or the approval "stales." The regulations provide for a one to sixty day extension to the approval, after which the property would presumably have to come back again to NJDEPE with a new application or a request for a letter of nonapplicability.

There should not be a sixty-day limit on negative declaration approvals. In the case of a business cessation, the negative declaration cannot be submitted or approved before all hazardous substances have been removed from the property. Once the substances have been removed and the negative declaration approved, that property must remain "ECRA-clear" until a new property use involving hazardous substances commences. In the case of a sale, the negative-declaration approval must remain valid for as long as the facts in the negative declaration remain accurate. The current sixty-day approval period is arbitrary, and puts unnecessary time constraints and extra paperwork on the industrial establishment and NJDEPE for a property that NJDEPE has already approved as clean. Those are some, not all, of the changes that must be made.

Turning to a wider view of ECRA, like other environmental legislation, it shares broad definitions of responsibility and liability. Liability can therefore be passed almost too easily; from tenant to landlord, or landlord to tenant, property owner to lender, present owner to previous owner, and so forth. These concepts can and do easily run afoul of the spirit of legal fairness.

Another anonymous businessman reported:

> A fundamental concept behind ECRA is that persons responsible for a property (owners and operators) should correct any environmental problems on that property before selling or moving. Unfortunately, many owners and operators are being held responsible for problems they did not create—problems which may have been caused fifty or one hundred years ago, before the days of careful environmental management. It is blatantly unfair to hold current owners responsible for previously undetected problems, which obviously occurred prior to the current ownership or occupancy. This unfairness, while not yet tested at the supreme court levels, has had its reverberations spread far and wide. It's not just a New Jersey problem.[3]

Other states are beginning to learn from New Jersey's environmental mistakes. A legislative committee in Illinois sent out questionnaires and queried numerous New Jerseyans who were familiar with the pitfalls of this legislation. After a careful review, they enacted their own legislation. In Illinois, the Responsible Property Transfer Act of 1988 keeps the state Department of Environmental Protection *out of real estate transactions.* "The act went into effect January 1, 1989," says Eric P. Canada, Director of Economic Development for the Illinois Chamber of Commerce, "We knew we didn't want what they have in New Jersey in Illinois."

Bernard Cohen, a physicist at the University of Pittsburgh, is quoted in a *Forbes* magazine article:

> Our government's science and technology policy is now guided by uninformed and emotion-driven public opinion rather than by sound scientific advice. Unless solutions can be found to this problem, the United States will enter the 21st century declining in wealth, power and influence . . . the coming debacle is not due to the problems the environmentalists describe, but to the policies they advocate.[4]

In June of 1991, Moody's Investor Service, Inc. published a document entitled, "The Environmental Risks and Corporate Quality Report." While this report focused on federal laws, it also discussed state regulations and their affect on companies and their credit ratings.

Further, the report gave estimates of obligations under the federal Comprehensive Environmental Response Compensation and Liability Act (CERCLA), as well as the Federal Resource Conservation and Recovery Act (RCRA). Its estimates of the costs of compliance were $25-$60 billion, and $23-$34 billion respectively.

> The mounting cost of compliance with federal environmental regulations could hurt credit ratings of some American companies, although it didn't think across-the-board downgrades would occur in industries . . . that a great deal of uncertainty remains about costs of environmental compli-

ance and clean-up of sites, and about whether some companies would bear a disproportionate share of the burden. It said credit ratings may come under pressure if uncertainties surrounding potential clean-up costs are resolved at greater cost than anticipated.

Among the industries affected are steel, chemical, mining, rubber and plastics, pulp and paper, electronics, pharmaceuticals and waste management; also included [are] casualty insurance companies with exposure to those companies as well as banks and thrifts that hold foreclosed industrial properties . . . Moody's expects increased pressure at the federal level to enforce existing regulations and stiffer regulations where current rules are considered ineffective. In addition, many states have passed tough clean-up laws that could compound environmental risks for some companies.[5]

The effect of heavier penalties and more stringent regulations will be felt by all companies in the United States. Larger companies may fare better than small companies, but this will be uneven in its application. Environmental costs will fall on chemical, processing, utilities, petrochemical and manufacturing the hardest, while companies in retail, distribution or marketing will be relatively unaffected.

Dan Scotto, analyst for Donaldson, Lufkin and Jenerette . . . reported that

In the next couple of years environmental clean-up costs will have a big tangible impact on budgets. The long-term effect will be to hurt utilities.

First Albany's Edward Lavarnway said, "Environmental costs will become a grave issue for many companies. There's a huge set of expenses looming out there but as yet no real appreciation of how much this will cost."[6]

In an old industrial state like New Jersey, such enormous costs of errant government policies have caused true hardships for innocent parties, and many owners and operators of old properties avoid triggering ECRA (and federal rules) in any way they can. ECRA was not "grandfathered," hence, the current property owner can be presented with the bill for environmental clean-up costs even though his property was polluted prior to his ownership! In this case, the current owner may be neither the "responsible party," nor "the industrial establishment" but under current implementation procedures, he is the party who must bear the brunt of the problem.

An owner whose land is polluted by third parties is not the "responsible party" but he may be caught in a trap. The cost of proving one's innocence under those circumstances is that of an innocent party trying to avoid the taint of guilt. The state does not have to prove guilt. The accused must prove his innocence. If he fails in this effort, he can be fined, held hostage to ECRA, and never be able to complete the transaction for which he filed, a transaction that will probably be killed by "delay."

Joint and several liability occurs when a landlord inherits a tenant's problem or a previous owner's or tenant's problem. The words "without regard to fault" imply deep pockets and show no regard for innocence or guilt. If drums were buried fifty years ago, and the current owner, bank, lessee, or lessor discovers them in the course of ECRA, is the discoverer the innocent or guilty party? Strangely, under various state and federal pollution laws, you can be guilty of a crime by not reporting pollution you find on your property, even if you didn't put it there. But, if you don't report it and the pollution is on your property, you, in essence, must turn yourself in!

One of the worst areas of pollution has been caused by the sloppy operations of our military. Many of our defense facilities have huge contamination problems. The desire to cut costs by closing military bases in 1990-1991 worked in reverse because of problems of toxic wastes. The federal government is seeking to save nearly $6 billion in the two decades after 1990. The closings, instead, will become disasters because they are creating moonscapes that could not be returned to economic viability. Keith Snyder reported in *The New York Times:*

> "If we don't get these [environmental] problems worked out, the base closure process will be a disaster for my community and 100 others," said Robert W. Holcomb, the mayor of San Bernardino, Calif., where Norton Air Force Base is scheduled to be shut in 1994. "The base will sit fallow, a no man's land, with no opportunity for our people to find employment."[7]

Elmer Schwartz, chairman of the East Orange-based Archie Schwartz Company, one of New Jersey's largest industrial real estate brokers, echoed similar sentiments.

> He spoke to his company's 175 person sales staff noting that the New Jersey economy is in a state of "devastation" not caused by foreign forces, but rather "the state's self-infliction of painful environmental laws that are beginning to grind local industry to a halt."
>
> According to Schwartz, millions of square feet of industrial real estate remain vacant and "without realistic environmental clean-up plans." Furthermore, he estimated that as many as 50,000 jobs have gone unfilled as a result of the stringent regulations and cumbersome enforcement.[8]

This is not a treatise on how to excuse or permit pollution. Environmental awareness by our defense agencies, businesses, and industries is, of course, a benefit to society. But our laws demonstrate a different reality. What is occurring in the business world is a studied approach on how to avoid unfair entrapment.

A small company needing $200,000 from a bank can't get it. If the property is ECRA-subject, the bank will request an environmental engineering study that will entail expensive legal fees, engineering time, and lab tests. Say it costs $50,000 and takes many months. It's a catch-22; you can't have the money you need until you perform, and you can't perform until you get the money!

Banks don't want to lend to ECRA-subject companies because of their lender liability risk. A bank can become secondarily liable for the clean-up costs if the loan or business fails to work out. If laws are going to hold a lender responsible for the liabilities of the borrower, there will simply be no loans. That's a practical fact! This process spells long-term economic ruin for any society that thinks these basic economic laws can be suspended.

At a recent luncheon, a very senior NJDEPE official and I argued over this point. Finally, in exasperation, the official said, "Siminoff, if banks won't lend business any money, then you should organize and force them to do so." That statement clearly showed his lack of understanding of this problem as well as the mindset of the environmental regulators.

But while New Jerseyans have not yet revolted over this duress, the anger of many individuals and companies grows. One can hardly blame Richard Sweet, the owner of a Burlington County concrete manufacturing company, for sounding bitter. Not only is business in the lagging construction market terrible, but at this time the State of New Jersey is also forcing his company to comply with a new set of underground storage tank regulations that is costing him a small fortune. "Compared to the mess in North Jersey, we're a pimple on a donkey's ass," he says. Our problem is minor, but I'm trying to do the right thing, even if these regulations are beyond comprehension in terms of complexity and cost."[9]

While the frustration among the targets of this overzealousness is growing, it is interesting to note that even some regulators are having second thoughts. Marvin Sadat, formerly head of the NJDEPE's Hazardous Waste Administration stated:

> The DEPE and EPA have maximum-level goals that are, in many instances, set at zero. They're perpetuating a myth that drinking water, for example, can be 100 percent risk free. It is politically expedient to say that their goal is zero, but it is scientific nonsense. I felt that way at the DEPE, and I feel that way now. Standards should be fully protective of public health, but make at least some scientific sense.
>
> New Jersey is the most regulated state in the nation, and the issue is a touchy one in many quarters, including the Governor's office, the halls of the New Jersey Business & Industry Association, and at the local gas station. In the last two years, the Garden State has certainly had its share of plant closings and company relocation announcements, and Sadat says that the importance of environmental concerns in each case is anybody's guess.[10]

Now regulators seem concerned about "standards." Agreement on standards is one of the major problems with ECRA and ECRA enforcement. Although standards for clean-up were supposed to be promulgated in 1984, they never were. The net result is that the standards to which business and industry will be held are those imposed by an assigned case worker and his manager and can vary on a case-by-case basis.

Suppose a man was stopped for speeding. The officer said, "Sir, you were speeding." "How fast was I going, officer?" "Well, I don't know, you just seemed to be going too fast." The officer would be saying in essence, "the speed limit is what I say it is." Environmental regulators have been given that kind of authority and power. From 1984 to 1991 this misuse of power continued unabated. One large company, Avon Products, challenged the DEPE on this enforcement practice. Avon won, but as of December 1991, the DEPE still hasn't enacted standards. Standards have been discussed and agreements could be reached but whether that will prove positive or negative is still uncertain.

Avon Products entered ECRA in 1985 when it contracted to sell its Belleville, New Jersey, facility to International Minerals and Chemicals Corporation. In 1986, Avon and the NJDEPE signed an ACO (Administrative Consent Order) and issued financial assurances totaling $1.5 million for the plant clean-up.

Since the DEPE had no standards, then or now, they ordered Avon to meet levels "dreamed up" by the case manager at that moment. The particular substance in question was P.C.B. (chlorinated biphenyls), which were used in electrical machinery prior to 1976. The NJDEPE ordered Avon to reduce this contaminant to 100 micrograms on the floor, machinery, and walls and to 250 micrograms for the roof.

Avon's engineering consultants stated that "it couldn't be done," and pointed out that the U.S. Environmental Protection Agency, that had promulgated standards, set them at 1,000 micrograms for floors. The Federal EPA had determined these levels to be safe, but New Jersey, with its overzealous ways, wanted a rate ten times greater on the floors, and forty times greater on the ceilings or roof.

Avon sued in federal court, stating that such standards were arbitrary and capricious, pointing out that the Federal Environmental Protection Agency guidelines were set after scientific studies.

The court, in a ruling by Judge Melvin Antell, agreed with Avon, ruling that the company could contest the clean-up plan developed by the NJDEPE in a court hearing. The court noted that even though ECRA was enacted in 1983 (effective 1/1/84), the DEPE had yet to adopt clean-up regulations as required. A case-by-case assessment is clearly nightmarish, since it just tests the missionary zeal (or lack thereof) of the individual case manager.

> "It has just led to a lot of confusion," said John Klock, an attorney who argued the case for Avon. "Without any standards, the regulators themselves are unregulated."
>
> Klock contended that the court ruling may finally force the state to address what those standards should be, and perhaps more important, how much money should be spent on cleaning up a site.
>
> At present, the department can set clean-up standards that have led to cases where a company has been forced to excavate soil from a site because hazardous waste has been detected in it, yet the same soil is considered safe enough to be used as a cover for a garbage dump in another state, he said.
>
> "Do we want to spend millions and millions of dollars to clean up something that poses no risk or harm to the public?"

Klock said. "Well, that is a question that at least ought to be debated by the public and business community."

Carla Israel, a lobbyist for the Chemical Industry Council of New Jersey, said the court's decision "just confirms to us the trend by the DEPE to ignore basic due process rights. You should get a full court hearing when a decision has implications that can run into million of dollars."[11]

What's the economic and societal result when rules become so arbitrary and capricious? A letter to the editor by Robert Frey of Phillipsburg, New Jersey, put it quite clearly:

> The push-down/pop-up effect of the New Jersey State Development and Redevelopment Plan (SDRP) has already manifested itself in Hoffman LaRoche's decision to locate its new Vitamin A plant out-of-state.
>
> After a glimpse at the New Jersey regulations it becomes obvious that a vitamin plant could not be built today in environmentally pristine Warren County.
>
> The State Department of Environmental Protection and Energy is the chief enforcing agency of the SDRP, according to the Commonwealth of New Jersey Forum held in Piscataway last month. This "common wealth" philosophy implies that all land belongs to the state no matter who owns it and pays taxes on it.
>
> Marx and Engels got this brainstorm too 140 years ago— and now after a long hard struggle with it both Russia and China are becoming disenchanted with socialism.[12]

One problem that is often forgotten is that within the United States all fifty states are in economic competition with each other. A state with higher taxes and with overzealous regulations will tend to drive business and jobs to more welcome places. Judging this movement is an inexact science. It is very difficult to obtain completely accurate statements from companies about their plant closings. The companies don't want to offend customers, suppliers, unions, banks, legislators, or stockholders. So they may "sugarcoat" plant closing announcements. One New Jersey company spokesman called it as he saw it.

> In a highly unusual announcement, the Chariot Group said it is closing its Republic Metal Products Inc. plant in Hillside, in part, because of New Jersey's tough environmental laws.
>
> Nearly 80 employees will be affected, according to a Chariot spokesman, although some might be retained in other operations. The company's earnings will be reduced during the fourth quarter as a result of the closing of the Union County maker of metal cabinets and sheetmetal parts.
>
> Chariot issued a statement citing reasons for the closing. They include the transfer of the company's customer base to other states and "the fact that New Jersey state environmental standards are more stringent than at its competitors' locations."
>
> Robert Saba, treasurer for the Chariot Group declined to specify the exact nature of the environmental problems at the plant.[13]

New Jersey's legislature has been aware of these many problems for some time, and various bills have been introduced to address some of the problems. But partisan political considerations have stalled the bills in the Senate, and no tangible reform is presently in sight. One reform bill, A-59, sponsored by Assemblyman Arthur Albohn, passed the assembly by a wide margin, 60-15, but was held up in and never released from a senate committee controlled by environmental extremists.

Rather than discouraging industry, we must all work collectively to change New Jersey's reputation from that of a harsh, overzealous environmental regulator to one that fairly regulates, encourages, and promotes clean industrial activities.

VII

Peculiar Results

The enforcement of ECRA has caused some truly peculiar results. Many of these are bizarre, some unintended, but taken together they all are negative. Perhaps the most strange of all is that the "environment," the subject of all this hysterical attention, has been shortchanged in the process.

Any law or set of laws that becomes abusive, simply sets in motion its own cancellation effect. Some historical examples are Prohibition, Prostitution, and Gambling. In New Jersey in 1989, a "Heavy Truck Tax" was instituted. No other state had one, so truckers purchased rigs in Pennsylvania or Delaware. Sales of heavy trucks plummeted 90 percent in New Jersey. The legislature repealed the truck tax, of course, but only after the damage had been done.

ECRA and its federal cousins have been monumental disasters, but these laws are more difficult to repeal and re-enact. Few officials have the political courage and are ready to go to battle with "Mother and Apple Pie." If perceived as "anti-environment," a politician can lose his office. While the need for reform cries out, political courage fades like an old photograph.

Hence, environmental overregulation has borne many strange results—all negative. Many of these effects were unintended, others were simply a result of poorly conceived legislation. In February of 1990, the Commerce and Industry Association completed a study of companies familiar with the ECRA process.

The survey found that, while companies were spending tens of thousands of dollars trying to comply with the complicated rules of ECRA, very little money was being spent cleaning up polluted property. The survey revealed that almost 80 percent of the money spent went toward filing and attorney fees, studies, consultants, and laboratories. Only 20 percent actually went toward cleaning up the pollution.

ECRA's costs are so excessive, expensive, and unfair that, instead of cleaning up New Jersey, it may be cleaning out the manufacturing sector of the economy instead. The study found that almost half the companies surveyed, or 46 percent, were changing their business plans or were considering moving out of state because of these stringent environmental laws.

It may be tempting to think that driving polluters out of the state is good. Unfortunately, many of these companies have been victims themselves of New Jersey's 200-year history of manufacturing. Much of the pollution found has not been caused by the present owner. The study revealed that innocent people are being driven to bankruptcy, and the tax base is being eroded as jobs leave the state. The survey found that approximately 75 percent of the companies found it difficult to obtain financing if they were ECRA-subject businesses.

The study was conducted over the course of a year and consisted of both written and oral interviews. Approximately 150 companies responded to the survey, out of more than 600. The Commerce and Industry Association of New Jersey is the state's largest regional business organization representing nearly 2,000 companies in Bergen, Essex, Hudson, Morris, Passaic and Union counties. Its "ECRA Task Force" performed the study. The study showed how far beyond the environment ECRA's efforts have reached.

Results of ECRA Survey

Started January 1, 1989—
Completed February 12, 1990

Total companies surveyed:

1.	Oral interviews	89
2.	ECRA applications randomly selected from NJDEPE list	313
3.	Mailed by real estate brokers and consultants to their ECRA clients	100
4.	Mailed by request of the ECRA Task Force	17
5.	Mailed by attorneys to their ECRA-experienced clients	<u>105</u>
	Total surveyed	624
	Returns—not deliverable	<u>–31</u>
	Total of net survey	593
	Total Respondents (Oral and Written)	155

Question 1:

Has your company been required to perform an environmental audit or ECRA review here in New Jersey?

_____Yes   _____No

Answer:

137   Respondents were requested to perform an ECRA review

9   Respondents were not required to perform an ECRA review but answered

1   No response

Question 2:

Did you find the ECRA filing process:_____Simple;

_____Complicated: _____Very Complicated?

Answer:

90%   "Very Complicated"

9%   "Complicated"

1%   "Simple"

Question 3:

What was the time required for compliance in conjunction with the various processes required by the Department of Environmental Protection?

_____Months;   _____Years;

Was this: _____Reasonable;   _____Unreasonable

Answer to Part One:

    60%   0-2 Years

    12%   2-3 Years

    28%   4 or More Years

Answer to Part Two:

    4%   Reasonable

    96%   Unreasonable

Question 4:

Please provide an estimate of your costs to date to comply with ECRA: ____Under $20,000; ____$20,000 – $50,000; ____$50,000 – $100,000; ____Over $100,000.

Answer:

    6%   Under $20,000

    10% $20,000 - $50,000

    20% $50,000 - $100,000

    64%   Over $100,000

What amount (or percentage) would you estimate was actually spent on clean-up costs?

    21%   Spent on clean-up costs

    79%   Spent on ECRA filing fees, lawyers, consultants, testing, etc.

Question 5:

With the time, money, and resources involved in complying with ECRA and other New Jersey Environmental Regulations, has your company been influenced to consider changing its business plans, closing down, or moving out of New Jersey?

Answer:

3%   Sold their businesses

2%   Bankrupt or in Chapter 11

12%   Not moving and/or changing their plans

37%   Did not answer, did not know, or had not reached any decision

46%   Were considering moving or changing New Jersey business plans and/or employment due to ECRA regulations. This percentage does not include the *"did not know or did not answer"* group

SURVEY NOTE

Of the companies stating that they planned to move from New Jersey, the following locations were most prominently mentioned as the places companies had chosen. They are listed in order of most mentioned selection: The Carolinas; Pennsylvania; New York; Texas; "The South"; several foreign countries.

Question 6:

If you answered "Yes" to any part of the above question, approximately how many employees would be affected?

_____Under 50   _____50 – 100   _____100 – 250

_____250 – 750   _____Over 750

Answer:

The following respondents said they *were* taking steps to move, curtail operations, open in another state, or otherwise affect their New Jersey operations because of ECRA experiences. These respondents stated that the following job losses could occur.

There were 2 categories of answers to this question:

1. Known job losses reported by the respondents to the survey were: 4,979 jobs.

Approximate job losses reported on the survey:

2. 8   Respondents losing 1 – 50 jobs

   22   Respondents losing 50 – 100 jobs

   13   Respondents losing 100 – 250 jobs

    5   Respondents losing 250 – 750 jobs

    1   Respondent losing 750 and more jobs

Potential job losses in question 2 above are estimated at 4,251 to 9,950. When combining answers 1 and 2, the survey uncovered a possible job loss effect of 9,230 jobs to 14,929 as expressed by the respondents. We do not know what percent of the total employment of the companies in the survey these job losses represent.

Question 7:

ECRA has reportedly caused lending problems for business. With regard to financing, loans, mortgages, etc., have you experienced:

a.   Problems with extended time involvement?

_____Yes   _____No

b.   Excessive additional expenses:_____Yes _____No

c.   Difficulty in financing your business due to ECRA?

_____Yes   _____No

Answer a.

Yes	70%	ECRA created problems with extended time involvement regarding financing their business
No	30%	ECRA did not create those problems

Answer b.

Yes	75%	ECRA created additional expenses regarding financing their business
No	25%	No additional expense

Answer c.

Yes	73%	ECRA created difficulties in financing business
No	27%	No additional difficulties

The strangest finding of the Commerce & Industry ECRA Study was that, after all the sound and fury of ECRA, an average of only 21 percent of the funds expended actually went to clean up the environment. In essence the state bureaucracy had succeeded in assembling regulations that were so complicated and led to so many "wild goose chases," that a 5-1 ratio existed between the costs of administering the program and the costs of cleaning up the sites.

The study showed that ECRA had far-reaching effects upon financing of businesses. While ECRA's aim was to make the purchase of property more secure, it actually worked in reverse. This occurs because it scares the purchaser as well as the seller. Mortgage money becomes a problem due to liability. If you can't *finance the ECRA costs, and/or can't sell your property, then you don't have purchasers or sellers participating.* The net experience of ECRA has been to depress the entire industrial real estate marketplace. It keeps many properties off the market; it does not free up parcels for sale!

When banks and lenders are held liable for clean-ups occurring through a mortgage lien, lending dries up. This process must be reversed, or a side effect of this regulation will be financial strangulation of the real estate markets. James W. Nelson, president of the Mortgage Bankers Association, was quoted as saying on July 10, 1991:

> "Several recent court decisions have held that, under Federal Superfund legislation, banks who acquire property through foreclosure and other defaults by borrowers are legally and financially responsible for environmental clean-up costs," Nelson said. He maintained that such concerns are contributing to the credit crunch by deterring commercial lenders from making some loans.
>
> "There is no doubt that the current state of the law has exacerbated lender uncertainty and, therefore, contributed as a major factor in the credit crunch," he told the Subcommittee on Policy Research and Insurance for the Committee on Banking, Finance & Urban Affairs.[1]

In April, 1992 the Federal E.P.A. adopted a rule change regarding Superfund cases. The new rule attempts to provide some comfort for banks who are just making a business loan, providing workout administration, or foreclosing. This rule lessens a bank's liability for clean-up costs.

However, the new rule does not assist any lender who participates in management, or assists in day-to-day decision making. If a lender participates in the client's environmental compliance or operational business decisions, he still would be liable for clean-up.

The above rule change was not extended to trusts or fiduciaries. In addition, it covers only Superfund cases and has not been extended to other Federal or State laws. While it is definitely a move in the right direction, the rule change has not gone far enough to restore confidence in the lending system regarding environmental liability.

Patrick O'Keefe, Executive Vice President of the New Jersey Builders Association put it this way:

> The suppression of building activity in New Jersey is directly attributable to an anti-growth attitude that has animated policymaking in Trenton for the past several years. An increasing array of regulatory restrictions has:
> -Increased the risks associated with development;
> -Inflated the industry's costs;
> -Decreased competitiveness.
> To illustrate: The state's approach to environmental protection is, by anyone's reckoning, highly inefficient. It is a system characterized by redundancy, subjectivity, and procrastination. As a consequence, the development approval process is highly improvisational and extremely expensive. While involving exaggerated risks, this approval process confers a significant premium on those projects that successfully navigate it. Simultaneously, the process tends to ration approvals, thereby impeding competition and removing price discipline from the marketplace.

Compounding this systemic inefficiency are policies that are more venturesome than elsewhere. We are told, for example, that ECRA (the Environmental Clean-up Responsibility Act), is a national model; but no other state has adopted similar legislation. Our freshwater wetlands law is touted as a trendsetter, but no other state has followed our lead. If imitation is the highest form of flattery, then our state's environmental policymakers should be humbled.

The state and local processes for the review of proposed development in New Jersey is tantamount to a war of attrition against those who must seek the manifold approvals required by law. While it is obvious that a dilatory review process costs private sector applicants time and money, contrived criteria are a subtle means of inflating agency workloads, thereby justifying staff increases.

Is it any wonder that the state's administrative agencies continue to report backlogs even though applications for building permits have dropped 75 percent over the past four years?

Surveys indicate that the median time needed to gain approval of a building project in New Jersey is in excess of three years! In the past twelve months alone, more than 1,000 bills relating to the building industry were introduced into the Legislature, while thousands of pages of new regulations were published. Can anyone prudently risk finite capital in such a climate of dilatory decision making and policy flux?[2]

In 1990 and 1991 our national banking system faced serious real estate loan problems, causing significant problems at our Savings & Loans, Commercial Banks, Insurance Companies and to our economy at large.

The troubles of our banks include a major undisclosed, yet dangerous collateral problem—"Environmental Lender Liability." This liability began with federal rules and has been made more pervasive by the four states that have adopted regulations even more stringent than the current federal obligations. These states, listed in order of the difficulty of their regulations, are: New Jersey (ECRA), California, Illinois, and Connecticut.

In New Jersey the title of a commercial property cannot be transferred without costly filing fees, lengthy paperwork, and exhaustive testing, all of which combine to formulate an environmental audit process. But how does this affect lenders? If a bank, mortgage company, lessor, or a repossessor (for example, a city, via a tax lien) seeks to recover their liened assets or collect their loan, they, themselves, become enmeshed in the environmental audit net because they become the new owner of the assets. The concept of "environmental lender liability" makes the current owner responsible for clean-up. You can become the current owner by foreclosing on a loan, or in a bank's case by even assisting in the operation of a client's business during financial difficulties.

Hence, if a bank forecloses on its loan or a city repossesses a property for back taxes, the foreclosing party picks up the liability as the new current owner. Then, in order to recover the loan, the foreclosing party is forced to clean up the property even though they didn't despoil it in the first place, a process that can take years.

Lenders have few choices. They can:

A. Lend more money to an unworthy credit risk so that the lender completes the environmental audit process himself. This throws good money after bad and is an example of bad banking!

B. Foreclose, taking the risk of needing large new sums to do the clean-up as well as years to perform it. Assets can be frozen in place for years.

C. Opt not to foreclose and/or write off the loan. The property is thus abandoned and left to the municipal government to foreclose for unpaid taxes.

D. In especially environmentally sensitive businesses (solvents, paint, chemicals, etc.) a lender may pump in new money keeping the client in business. This choice only compounds the fiscal troubles, but postpones environmental clean-up.

The result is that banks can be stuck with commercial, industrial, business, and real estate loans that cannot be made whole, through no fault of the lender. In our national zeal to clean up the environment, we have failed to see the dangerous consequences of regulatory overkill. We only have created future financial time bombs for lenders as well as our economy.

Lenders are carrying thousands of questionable loans that are not yet bad but may not ever be recoverable. At the same time credit is impossible to obtain if one is a small manufacturer who could subject his lender to this potential future liability. Only large companies can survive this tightening process.

The picture that evolves is one of federal and state environmental regulations that *in themselves could continue to force the collapse of many lending institutions.* In addition pressure is created on older manufacturing cities that also pick up this liability upon tax lien foreclosures. Officials of several of New Jersey's largest cities have told me that they will no longer foreclose on tax liens for environmentally sensitive properties. It is frightening that while these liabilities can destroy loans and even an innocent lender in the process, the banks, the general public, and the regulators may be totally unaware of this looming iceberg. The public may think that once the banking crisis is over—it's over for good. This is not so, because it is the "off-the-books" liabilities that hit like a shot in the dark, at a time when you least expect it.

Another side effect of ECRA is its destruction of the Urban Renewal process. Older New Jersey cities are unable to attract development or developers. As Steffan Gable, Director of Mercer County (N.J.) Economic Development has aptly stated:

> There is a real need to have funds available to conduct analysis on existing and former industrial sites primarily in our cities . . . but also throughout New Jersey.
>
> Since ECRA (Environmental Clean-up Responsibility Act) was established, some potential property purchases by both investors and users have not proceeded because of the uncertainty of *potential* unknown clean-up costs. In some instances, properties were or are in bankruptcy, and funds are not available to conduct the initial investigation to determine if any clean-up is required. In some cases, potential buyers are unwilling to take the financial risk of investing in a study which might result in a total loss of their investigative capital. In the City of Trenton alone, we can identify six properties with tax arrearages totaling nearly $1 million.
>
> The lack of productive reuse can be directly traced to ECRA issues, both real and perceived. Part of the problem is

fear of the unknown. This situation has stifled the potential purchase of *some sites* that *might not require any clean-up,* stifled the purchase of sites that *might require* financially feasible clean-up and inhibited the potential discovery of other sites that *might need major Super Fund participation.*

In many instances, both buyer and seller are reluctant or unable to fund the cost of studies. What remains are unutilized or under-utilized buildings and land. These buildings are functionally obsolete and less desirable because of their structural configuration, the degree of disrepair, the perceived notion that reinvestment might make the project non-competitive and non-financiable by conventional means. These factors ultimately translate into costs . . . .

The bottom line is we must get properties put into productive use, create jobs, foster capital investment, tax revenues and most importantly get sites cleaned up.[3]

ECRA's intent was to convince potential buyers of New Jersey industrial real estate that their purchase was "clean." Unfortunately, it has done exactly the opposite. There are no buyers! An article in the *Easton Express* of Easton, Pennsylvania stated the sad emotions of ECRA:

> Ed Croot, an industrial real estate broker in Warren County, stands in a bleak parking lot near a former tannery, looks to the pouring heavens, raises his arms and cries: "What in God's name was it all for?"
>
> His unanswered question echoes off the building, one of two industrial properties in Hackettstown he has tried his hardest to sell. But the deals triggered a controversial New Jersey law called ECRA—the Environmental Clean-up Responsibility Act.
>
> The law has left Croot, and others like him, shaking their heads and wondering why.

The idea behind the law is simple: Prevent buyers from purchasing polluted property.

But critics like Croot contend that this simple idea with the complex bureaucracy behind it is hurting business in New Jersey. They say the intent of the law is good, but its execution is fraught with excessive fees and lengthy delays.

(Many business owners contacted for this story refused to be identified, claiming the DEPE is vindictive toward its critics, a charge the DEPE denies.)

Croot isn't as resigned—he's angry. In a position paper penned during sleepless early morning hours Croot wrote:

"ECRA has been given a precious diamond facade that appears as sugar and spice and everything nice. But, cleverly camouflaged and masked behind this picturesque facade is a vicious, cruel, sadistic wolf in sheep's clothing, that has no mercy for its helpless victims."[4]

The absurdity of misguided regulations can be clearly seen by the case of a large manufacturing company, and their ultimate decisions. This concern, Ingersoll-Rand, is a very large New Jersey employer. They own a substantial piece of industrial property along Route 22 in Phillipsburg (Warren County), N.J. This property is located between Route 78 and Easton, Pennsylvania, on New Jersey's Western border.

The property has been an industrial site for more than 100 years. Ingersoll's management felt that they were faced with an impossible "catch-22" situation. They wanted to reduce the size of this particular plant, and rent or sell the remaining property to others. If they kept several operations there and turned the remainder into an industrial park, everyone (including the community) would benefit. Jobs would remain, taxes would be paid, and the local economy buoyed.

However, a *change of use* (change of SIC Code) could trigger ECRA onto the entire property (even unused sections). While there were rumored to be several interested tenants, management couldn't rent the property to them for several reasons: (A) It could trigger ECRA; (B) If the tenant rents the property from Ingersoll, he can become "jointly and severally liable, without regard to fault" for the past 100 years of industrial usage. This could occur even though the tenant was not a polluter, and just arrived on the premises.

What do you do when ECRA prevents a (economically justified) sale, or rental, due to its costs and length of time, and its daisy chain of liability? You change the game.

The company decided to whittle down employment, tear down more than 25 buildings, and just keep a few operating. As the plant manager stated:

"We were stymied from selling because any transfer would trigger the ECRA law," according to Walter J. Schmidt, general manager of I-R's Engineered Pump Division. "So we decided instead to tear the buildings down."

Similarly, the company cannot sell the vacant land for new industry, even though Phillipsburg and Warren County are hungry for jobs.

"God knows what you'd find underneath the ground after 100 years, although to my knowledge, there's nothing there," Schmidt says.

"Any problems we have had on our site, we've cleaned up. We have always operated according to environmental laws. But we've been manufacturing here since 1908. The laws have changed over the years."

The newly formed Phillipsburg Economic Development Committee, a group of businessmen drawn from the community, has made ECRA reform one of many goals for the coming year, says Chairman Richard Daubert. This is partly due to the Ingersoll situation.

"It's just having such a negative impact instead of positive support," he says. The group will work to make the laws less restrictive and plans to host a workshop to educate local business owners about the environmental law. Most people, Daubert says, have never heard of ECRA."[5]

The results of the Ingersoll Rand situation are all negative: (A) Jobs lost; (B) Property remains unusable; (C) Real estate tax payments are greatly reduced to Phillipsburg, (D) The community suffers economic loss and will continue to do so as long as the property remains fallow. Absolutely no one has benefited from this pathetic scenario. Clyde Folley, Vice Chairman of Ingersoll Rand, put it clearly:

> We know all the red tape involved, we know the regulations we require, we know what ECRA means when you have to do something, how it can take you two years to get a permit to put a paintbooth into a factory. We know what all of this is costing business and we're not the polluters. We're not out [just] to make a profit and pollute the world. And I don't just mean Ingersoll Rand.[6]

A letter to the editor of *The Star Ledger,* entitled "Road Sale Plan Suffers Major Flaw," shows more of these strange pathways:

> "There's been a lot of talk recently regarding New Jersey's Department of Environmental Protection and Energy and Commissioner Scott Weiner's promise to impose the same enforcement standards on other government agencies as DEPE imposes on private industry. Recent events will give Weiner ample opportunity to demonstrate his resolve in keeping his promises and, ironically, it will be the Governor himself who provides the forum.
> Now that its legal counsel has approved the deal, the New Jersey Turnpike Authority can go ahead with the Governor's

plan to sell some state highways to the authority for $400 million.

If Weiner keeps his promise, there won't be much of that $400 million left after the Environmental Clean-up Responsibility Act (ECRA) rules are applied.

ECRA demands that before properties can legally change hands, the owner must certify that the property complies with minimum health standards. If it fails certification, it must be cleaned up before the sale. Has anyone thought about all the fuel, brake dust, engine oil, and cargo spillage that has been washed off to the sides of these highways over the years they have been in use? Has anyone considered the expense of sinking test wells deep into the ground on both sides of the highways for all those miles, or the dollars that will be consumed collecting and testing all those samples? Has anyone factored in the cost of removing contaminated soil, shipping it out of state, burning it and replacing it?

To one degree or another, the shoulders and properties adjacent to both sides of these roads are contaminated by crankcase drippings and asbestos brake material, both known carcinogens. That same soil also contains concentrations of tetraethyl lead, an anti-knock compound used in gasoline for generations and whose threats to health are also well-documented. Mind you, we haven't even begun to discuss ground contamination caused by cargo spillage from accidents involving tank trucks!

The curtain has yet to rise on what promises to be some very entertaining comedy. Yet many industry leaders are already laughing up their sleeves in anticipation that the Governor might have to spend $500 million in clean-up costs in order to get his $400 million "profit." For a change the shoe is on the other foot and the audience loves it.

It will be interesting to see how Weiner and the Governor deal with this. Will the state do what so many individuals have been forced to do: Abandon the property? Will Florio dictate to Weiner to "do as I say, not as I do?" Will the commissioner compromise his integrity and go along with his boss or will he resign in a demonstration of self-righteous indignation?

One thing is for certain, the Governor is denied the one option most exercised by industry—he can't leave the state!"[7]

On June 30, 1991, Governor Florio signed the 1991-1992 New Jersey State Budget. The new budget included the sale of New Jersey-owned roads to the Turnpike Authority. Will the State or Federal Government enforce environmental rules on this transaction?

In September 1991, I sent the following letter to *The Star Ledger,* calling attention to the effect of proposed environmental regulations on homeowners.

New Jersey businessmen have lived through many regulatory travails during the past decade. A whole parade of anti-business and anti-job regulations, such as ECRA, Clean Water, N.J. Help (Proposed), etc. have combined to make us the most anti-business state in the nation. Constitutional protections of due process, private property, self-incrimination, search warrants, to name a few, have been stripped from businessmen like bark from a tree—without a fight!

Unfortunately, environmental protectionism has given way to "extremism." Now, New Jerseyans are confronted with a convoluted web of complex regulations for: moving dirt, carting away leaves and grass clippings, selling their business (this can take years), cutting down trees on one's property, repairing one's septic tank, etc., etc.—what's left?

The NJDEPE has just adopted an expanded set of regulations . . .which will now apply to all "persons responsible for a discharge." *This will affect virtually every business and every homeowner in the State of New Jersey!*

In addition to the widening of their regulations to include homeowners, a considerably expanded list of hazardous substances has been promulgated. The new list incorporates and now includes, for example, [acetic] acid (found in vinegar), saccharin, sodium nitrate (a preservative), nicotine and common fertilizers.

Also, a broad definition of a discharge will now become existent. The NJDEPE has specifically noted that it does *NOT exempt homeowners* or small business from its notorious discharge reporting requirements.

Although the U.S. Constitution calls for protection against "self-incrimination," the NJDEPE does not generally recognize established constitutional protections and continues this course in its lists of pronouncements.

Hence, any citizen affected is required under DEPE regulations to self-incriminate himself. He is to notify the New Jersey Spill Hotline within 15 minutes, and confirm in writing a discharge within 30 days from occurrence.

In response to a comment concerning whether a homeowner spilling gasoline while refueling a lawn mower must report a spill, the NJDEPE responded that "(a) spill of gasoline by a homeowner may be reportable, dependent upon the circumstances of the spill. If the spill is onto the lands or into waters of the State, it is a discharge and must be reported. If the gasoline spills onto a surface such as concrete from which it can be cleaned up or removed so it does not enter the lands or waters of the State, it is a leak which need not be reported." In response to comments that there could be a number of absurd results including requiring reporting of fertilizing of a lawn when phosphorous is an ingredient in the fertilizer, the reportability of a throat lozenge which may contain a minor amount of phenol, and dripping of oil from cars onto roadways because the road may drain to a storm sewer, the NJDEPE responded that it *"wants to be aware of all discharges that are occurring within New Jersey."*[8]

Anyone who has dealt with the NJDEPE and its encompassing web of regulations knows what will happen when that organization next invades the lives of homeowners. While there is no freedom to pollute, New Jerseyans better somehow find the courage to tell their legislators "we have had it." If we don't—the day is fast approaching when *you will need a permit* (from the NJDEPE) *to sell your house or farm.* This is beginning to evolve as a series of individual permits: radon, septic, water well, spill reports, etc.

I testified before a legislative committee regarding ECRA during the summer of 1988. The gentleman who preceded me told an unforgettable story.

He had purchased a ten-acre parcel of land in southern New Jersey. This parcel of land had previously been grass, trees, and unutilized pasture. He erected a 15,000 square foot building in which the company manufactured a nonpolluting line of industrial products. He put in an attractive planting of shrubberies, a new lawn, driveways, and parking. In order to properly level and landscape, the site required about twenty dump-truck loads of topsoil, which was purchased from a local grain farmer who was located one mile down the road.

Two years after his topsoil purchase, another business transaction triggered ECRA. His lawyer told him that the company would "whiz through in 90 days," knowing that his property was formerly clean, (nonindustrial) and that he and his employees had kept the property in immaculate condition. The business did not pollute; it stored very few toxic chemicals, and the inventory was clean, organized, and visually attractive.

The company filed the papers, paid the fees, and received a visit from the NJDEPE case manager. The case manager requested that soil and water tests be undertaken. Over the next several months, the owner complied with this and all other requests. He felt that this would be a short-lived intrusion into his business life.

When the test results were received, the owner was informed that he *had sustained significant contamination* of his soil. The owner believed this impossible since the area was previously a clean meadow and contained very old trees prior to his purchase. He was certain that no commercial activities had been conducted on the site.

The contaminant was soon identified as an agricultural pesticide. Soon, it became clear that the topsoil trucked in from the nearby farm contained certain residual pesticides that had been used by the farmer.

The owner requested a meeting with the case manager. He told the manager that the problem was found. "We will remove the soil and take it back to the farm." The DEPE official said, "No, that is impossible. In New Jersey, pesticides of this type are legal on a farm, but not legal in the soil of an industrial establishment! The soil will have to be treated as hazardous waste." As the owner explained to the legislative committee, this meant "that it would cost him several hundred thousand dollars to do so. If the soil were to be treated as a hazardous substance, placed in individual drums, and transported to Ohio, this made no sense." He further stated that he didn't have the working capital to accomplish this, since it was totally unexpected. "Why can't I just take it back to the farm where it's legal?" he asked.

At that moment, a reporter seated at the side of the room, looked very perplexed, raised his pencil in the air, and in an unusual spasm of energy called out:

"Mr. Chairman, Mr. Chairman." The Chairman turned, looking at him sternly and said, "What is it?"

"Mr. Chairman, I am greatly pained by this story. The pesticides described here are legal on the farm, on the corn that we eat, but not legal on the company's grass, what's going on?"

The Chairman banged his gavel three times and said, "It's time for a recess."

It surely was, I remember thinking. My testimony was not quite as illuminating as the "farm story."

VIII

That's Another Agency's Problem

This chapter describes one ECRA case.* The case has lasted four years, nearly bankrupted a company, caused the reduction of fifty jobs, and exceeded one million dollars in cost. The story is not yet over, and the company may yet seek bankruptcy protection, having been so drained by the experience. Less than 15 percent of the cost was expended for removal of oil-contaminated soil. Nearly 85 percent of the expenditures were for state filing fees, legal and consultant costs, testing, management time, etc.

The company had been located in New Jersey for nearly fifty years. Its business would commonly be described as a

---

*This chapter is based on a real ECRA case. Management permitted full access to their books, records, invoices and tally sheets. Employees were interviewed as well as the company's consultants, lawyers, and management. Due to their near bankruptcy from ECRA and fear of NJDEPE retaliation for speaking out, the company requested complete anonymity. Hence, changes have been made to conceal corporate identity.

machine shop. The company had been located at its southern New Jersey site for more than ten years and had taken considerable care of its environment. In terms of employee consideration, community caring, and environmental concerns, the company and its management were leaders. The company participated in civic projects, prison release labor programs, use of handicapped workers, and employee family participation. Management naively believed they would sail through ECRA because they ran a clean business and were reasonable people.

Several members of the company's management were World War II veterans who believed that no law or regulation could be as bad as ECRA's reputation. They had fought for this country and believed in its principles. They entered the case "telling their government everything they knew," while assisting all DEPE personnel and inspectors. They believed that cooperation and openness would speed their case through the system. "We believed we had nothing to hide," stated the president.

The company's environmental consultants looked over the premises and felt from the beginning that "everything [could] be done for about $100,000." While this was a considerable amount of money, it could be afforded, and initially was viewed as a way "to perform the company's civic duties." Hence, the company filed its papers without any deep concern.

The fact that the final tally would nearly bankrupt the company was never considered to be a possibility. How could that happen? How could concerned citizens be so wrong?

The first error made by any businessman is the belief that ECRA is a "clean-up law." No, it is a mission being enforced by environmental crusaders who are out to teach lessons to suspected polluters. That one is not a polluter is immaterial. In the mind of such a missionary those on the other side must be converted. "Every business must pollute. There are no innocent parties."

In 1349 A.D. an English Philosopher, William of Ockham, said that entities should not be multiplied unnecessarily. He promoted the idea of simplicity and suggested that complex solutions to problems are only to be used when simplicity proves impossible. Unfortunately, "Ockham's razor" as the principle is known, is quickly dispelled when one enters the ECRA process. The regulators' onerous and complicated web becomes the dragon that is impossible to satiate.

The historic use of land and surrounding areas are not a factor. The agency treats each industrial site as a "mini-Superfund" site. But it makes no sense to clean up an industrial property to such low contaminant levels when, a year or two later, it will be back to its previous levels if a business continues to operate there.

This case entered ECRA as a continuing operation. In other words the business would keep its operations "as is, where is." The company was not about to turn its industrial site into a shopping center or an apartment house complex; it would continue as a "machine shop." Machine shops use oil, solvents, and cleaners. The NJDEPE perceives the site as pristine even though this business was going to remain exactly where it was under new ownership. The buildings were not being knocked down for a change in use.

The first thing the company did was to hire a lawyer and consultant. The attorney prepared and filed the "General Information Submission" GIS-001 (see Appendix 3). This was followed by the "Site Evaluation Submission" SES-002 (see Appendix 3). The cost of preparation and legal fees was approximately $10,000. The state required $7,500 as a submittal fee with the application, since it included ground water monitors. The state filing fee, paid throughout the process, is for each form filed and serves no legitimate purpose other than the fee "is required."

The completed SES-Sampling Plan proposal ran over three hundred $8^{1}/_{2} \times 11$ pages. It consisted of forty pages of sampling results, mainly concerned with possible oil spillage. Since all machines, even sewing machines, use oil, the search for oil spillage has enlarged ECRA to monumental proportions. This official concern is true even when drinking water and run-off are not compromised. The next area of the submission included 125 pages of investigation from "storm sewers to catch basins, to drains, loading docks, transformers, and run-off waters, etc."

Section Three consisted of seventy-nine pages entitled "Appendices." This attached material ranged from "Soil Boring Logs to Soil Laboratory Results." Following this, are topographical maps, locations to be checked, and various tables, which constitutes another fifty pages! The cost for this site plan preparation totaled nearly $40,000 in preparation and environmental consulting fees, without accruing management time.

At this point the president realized that due to the complexities encountered, ECRA would not be a cakewalk. The site was suddenly being turned into a "mini-Superfund." This filing was only the warning flare. The honeymoon with the concept of benevolent regulation was about to end. It was becoming clear that the government agency's mission had some other purpose than simply site clean-up.

Sometime after that filing the NJDEPE case manager arrived at the site and walked the property. It was initially agreed to drill two water wells for underground monitoring, to perform soil sampling, and to check certain areas for contamination.

An "Interim Report of Clean-up" was then prepared. The mini-Superfund operation had now begun. Partial excavations were proposed under the parking lots, fuel tank areas, at storm sewers and drains, entrance and exit areas, storage areas, abandoned unused tanks, and all drainage easements, streams, and water run-off areas. This interim report totaled over one hundred pages and cost more than $25,000 for preparation. In addition more than five employees and two management people were now working on all or part of the case. One person with an administrative background was appointed exclusively to perform the supervisory function. The process had become a mental depressant to all employees who were fearful of losing their jobs. The continued cash expenditures, brain drain, and mental pressure caused by the ECRA process caused the company's business to decline. To get through the process, the company would have to slim down—reduce certain people, sell equipment, and try to raise cash for the environmental costs. ECRA now looked like a $300,000 expenditure, three times the original estimate, and this sum still on preliminaries. The state, vendors, consultants, and laboratories all knew that this was a crushing financial experience. So they insisted on prompt payment. They knew the process bankrupts companies. If a contractor held up work, the company could be fined by the NJDEPE.

The company's bank, which had financed its operations for nearly fifteen years, grew edgy and relationships hardened. Because of their possible secondary liability if the company's efforts fail, many banks attempt to pull out of loans at this juncture. However, the company's bank continued with them.

It was now necessary to prepare an "At Risk Sampling and Clean-up Plan." This 150 page document cost over $50,000 (the company was now accruing all costs). This report dealt with: Summary and Overview; Remedial Action Proposals (thirty pages), Cost Estimates, Scheduling, and Exhibits and Appendices.

Remember that while this work was going on, the practical environmental problem was possibly *some oil contamination* from previous machine shop activities. In addition, there existed the possibility of spilled solvents in the ground. Once a company is in ECRA, however, it can be pressured into testing for almost everything including off-site problems (pre-1991), and rivers and streams that are adjacent to or on the property. The threat of heavy fines is always there, and you are reminded constantly of the dire consequences of noncooperation. These threats can be extortionary, and management was fearful of the consequences if they fought back.

In the middle of the process it was determined by monitoring a well that a substance that had never been used on the property previously had been found in the groundwater. Obviously, it must have originated off-site. The substance was a fuel additive, but nothing relating to this additive was ever located on or near this location.

Being in ECRA, the property owners had to prove their innocence. They were guilty, via property ownership, hence an effort had to be made to prove where the outside pollution had originated. This investigation required the employment of a new consultant called a "hydro-geologist."

It took six and a half months, four new wells (at $5,000 each), hundreds of man-hours, maps and studies of flow direction, etc., to prove the company's innocence. Eventually, at a cost of nearly $50,000 and 125 pages of documentation, the NJDEPE agreed that the fuel additive contamination was indeed from off-site. The company was now permitted to resume its ECRA travail.

A "Final Groundwater Monitoring Plan" was prepared and submitted next. This document was only twenty-five pages, and cost about $10,000 to prepare. By this juncture the company had to reduce employment by another fifteen persons and was on an asset sales program to raise additional cash in order to pay for these costs. The case was nearly two years old, and, yet, not one yard of soil had been removed or remediated. The bank had begun to "rattle sabers"; no more financing would be entertained, and personal signatures were requested by the bank for its assurance (these were never given).

Indeed, it was found that oil had crept into several areas around the facility, and this oil-soaked dirt had to be removed.

What this meant in practical terms, was that the oil-tinged dirt had to be removed in individual barrels and trucked out of state where it was buried in ex-missile silos or some similar place. The barrels could not remain in New Jersey. The barrels could not be encapsulated (buried in concrete or contained) at the site. The dirt could not remain, even if it had no effect on water or residences. For practical reasons a company cannot clean the soil and put it back in the hole. Further, you can't take soil from another part of your facility and fill in a hole elsewhere. The reason for this aberration is a practical one. In order to put dirt back into an excavation, it must be clean. How clean? That is the rub. If a company attempts to put its own dirt back in the hole, then they must prove it is without contamination. This requires a significant amount of testing and the involvement of time. It is far cheaper and more practical to purchase clean washed gravel (or certified clean dirt) and utilize that instead of using your own soil or stones. This is somewhat strange, but it is a side effect produced by the ECRA thought process.

The company hired an approved hazardous waste contractor and trucker who (in their white suits) excavated and removed eight truckloads of dirt, barrel by barrel. Most of the dirt was only slightly contaminated. Spilled oil doesn't travel far underground. Each truck contained individually sealed white barrels. Carefully prepared manifests were executed, and dirt removal proceeded without a hitch. The destination of this convoy was Ohio. The cost—about $100,000.

Four times during the travail the ultimate in bureaucratic harassment occurred. Management called it "the case manager change." Since ECRA is handled on a case-by-case basis (without statewide standards) each case manager had his own particular emphasis and personal standards. If a case manager changed, a new emphasis or bias began. Each time a change occurred, the company received a letter requesting a delay to "get acquainted with the file and the subject matter." These delays took from thirty to ninety days each. Of course the case manager change always seemed to occur during an important segment of the process.

The most glaring example occurred between case manager three and four. Case manager three declared the "company to be out of the process." "You've completed everything I've requested, and I will now be working on your final paperwork and declaration." Management was thrilled. "It was like being let out of jail," the president said.

The company, tired and weary but still in business, waited. About sixty days after this pronouncement they received a letter from case manager four who was just assigned to the project. Management explained to the new case manager that they were finished, but case manager four said he would have to come up and "just look things over, since I am new on the case." Looking back, management agrees that they should have launched a counterattack at this point. But, they were lulled to sleep by the statement made by case manager three that the company was out of the ECRA process.

Case manager four arrived, fresh, and with a new bent. He stated that he could not sign off just yet but would like six more wells drilled in a new area to check on off-site contamination possibilities. Just six more wells at $5,000 each. The company protested. Management told the case manager that "we are running out of money, teetering on bankruptcy; we might have to shut down . . . over 100 jobs would be lost if you push us further." The president said, "we are now hanging on by our financial fingernails."

"If your business fails, that's another agency's problem," said the environmental official. "I still want more wells drilled." Management again capitulated—more wells were drilled. More tests were done; the site had now become a chemical laboratory. The state had won. The new case manager saw the manicured lawns, beautiful flowering azaleas, shrubs, and flagstone walks as merely figments of the imagination. He knew in his callous environmental heart that these guys were hiding contamination. It had to be there. All businessmen were polluters. He just knew it. Case managers one, two, and three just didn't find it.

After more tests, the same oil-soiled dirt proved to be the only item found. At this juncture the total costs were more than one million dollars (see chart); over fifty people had lost

ECRA CASE CHART

Summary	Estimated Cost	Approximate Costs W/Accruals	Approximation of Paperwork Pages
1. Original Estimate	$100,000		
1. Original Estimate		$ 24,500	10
2. Filing GIS-001		40,000	300
3. Filing SES-002		25,000	100
4. Interim Report		50,000	150
5. At Risk Sample Plan		50,000	125
6. Off-Site Contamination		10,000	25
7. Ground Water Monitoring		100,000	6
8. Dirt Removal			190
9. PreClean-Up Plan			200
10. Soil & Ground Water Investigation		900,000	50
11. Soil Clean-up Report			225
12. Final Clean-up Report			125
13. Final Monitoring and Sample Plan			
14. Employee, Management, Legal, and All Other Costs			
		Total: $1,199,500	1,506

their jobs (in cutbacks), and nearly 1500 pages of reports had been produced. The company's relations with its bank, employees, and community soured. Of the total costs, less than 15 percent actually went to environmental clean-up, the removal of oil-soiled dirt taken away in clean white barrels. The company remains in business, now heavily in debt. Management wishes to move from New Jersey and to be treated fairly, somewhere, once again. The site is still a machine shop. Yes, management is now more environmentally cautious. Any future contamination will be small. But the company also was careful prior to ECRA. The experience has sapped the business of its finances, vibrancy, and momentum.

IX

The Agency's Big Brother

Those readers who have been mired in ECRA probably cannot conceive of anything worse. But all who know Murphy's Law would immediately sense that there will be more strident scenarios.

Let us examine the issue of "wetlands protection." Wetlands has been jumped on by the entire environmental movement as an item of majestic importance.

"Don't you want to drink clean water?" is the practiced retort when one questions this stance. That we must protect our water, has no argument. But how much of your freedom do you wish to give up for water protection?

After examination of the issues, it will be clear that we can have pure water without sacrificing our basic freedoms.

As with ECRA, or its brothers and sisters, once environmental bureaucrats get a mandate that contains as much fertile ground for mischief as wetlands, they "go to town."

Wetlands regulations being proposed by the U.S. Army Corps of Engineers, the Federal EPA, and various New Jersey regulations are mind-boggling. If property is federally designated as a wetlands site, then the owner must have an Army Corps of Engineers permit before doing any site work. In New Jersey the environmentalists have gone one step further and have issued separate protection plans for fresh water and salt water wetlands. Regulations can be very abusive and, of course, are retroactively applied with few if any examples of grandfathering.

In May 1991, the NJDEPE issued an order that effectively revoked the permits of more than twenty statewide projects that were previously excepted from wetlands legislation passed in 1989-1990, since most were already under way. In a sensible fashion they were grandfathered. These exceptions were confirmed by the New Jersey Attorney General's Office in late 1990. It made good sense to grandfather projects that were moving ahead prior to the law's effective date.

But six months later more than twenty of these projects had their grandfathered exceptions withdrawn. Substantial time and money had been expended by all of the land owners and developers because dozens of permits had to be obtained.

The withdrawal of a grandfathered permit can be difficult enough, but consider the landowner's next step. Does he sue the state? Can he sell the land? Does a property owner have any rights at all if he finds his property is partially designated as wetlands? Referring to the above situation, the Morris County (N.J.) *Daily Record,* reported:

The state Department of Environmental Protection and Energy told 26 developers yesterday that their projects are in jeopardy because a review of wetlands regulations revealed they had erroneously been given permission to build . . .

"DEPE is committed to consistent administration of the Freshwater Wetlands Protection Act of 1987," Weiner said. It became clear that DEPE had made a mistake in implementing the law . . . and recognizes its obligations to make decisions that are open, fair and consistent.

"I appreciate the interests of those who apparently received improper exemptions and now may be experiencing a hardship," he continued. "At the same time, DEPE could not let stand these decisions that were so obviously contrary to state law."

"The law prohibits development in freshwater wetlands without a pressing public need or lack of alternative sites," Assistant DEPE Commissioner John Weingart said. "Those who are permitted to build must create two acres of wetlands at another location for each acre destroyed by the project," he said.[1]

On the surface, wetlands protection sounds reasonable and plausible, but those administering it were bitten by the "ECRA Virus." If it is unreasonable to deny someone the right to build on his property, which he has owned for many years and has permits, then be prepared for the next level of environmental terrorism.

What entity other than industry uses water in large quantities? The answer is—farming. We have been led to believe that farmers enjoyed many exemptions since they grow food for all of us. Well, the family farm is now feeling the sting of ECRA's big brother—wetlands hysteria! The following is from the *Farm Journal:*

"Missouri farmer Allen Moseley's fine for building an illegal levee on his land is $14 million, and grows bigger by the day. "It works out to another $1 million every 40 days," he says.

In Colorado, Larry Gerbaz faced $40 million in fines for rebuilding a levee after the Corps refused to say whether he needed a permit. After much anguish in the Gerbaz family and negative press regarding the high fine, EPA decided to settle for several thousand in fines.

Cranberry grower Joe Darlington tried to accommodate the Army Corps of Engineers by filing all the government permits and environmental studies required by state and federal laws; but the process has taken three years and he still doesn't have permission to replace a 22-acre bog in his family's Browns Mills, N.J., cranberry operation.

"It's frustrating when you think of yourself as a farmer concerned about water quality and all the things that environmentalists favor," says Darlington, who is asking permission to swap a bog on the state's list for historic preservation with one in another location. "But as soon as you start the process, you are treated as if you want to rape the land."

"What angers cranberry producers most is that their farming operations are frozen in the status quo," says Steve Lee, a spokesman for the American Cranberry Growers Association. Demand for their crop is booming, but growers are not allowed to expand acreage or adopt modern technology because of the wetlands policy, he says. "If you're in an industry that doesn't change—you won't be able to meet the competition from foreign growers. This is crazy."[2]

The zealots who would revoke a permit six months after granting it, are the same missionary types who are going to war against farmers.

Man cannot live on this planet without making some use of its resources. That certainly doesn't give anyone the right to dirty or despoil them. On the other hand, the cloak of environmentalism doesn't give anyone the right to use water, air, or soil, as a reason to strip others of their individual rights. Unfortunately, agencies involved in environmental protection compete. A law is passed, the U.S. EPA writes its regulations, then the Corps of Army Engineers writes its regulations. Individual states like New Jersey then feel compelled to surpass both of these agencies. The poor citizen/taxpayer/property owner/farmer is caught in the middle.

The problem with retroactive environmental regulations is that they often start with impossible premises. Farms and factories have been operated for over three hundred years in the United States. Yes, some have despoiled the environment, but if wetlands were farmed continuously for one hundred years by the same farm family, should they be deprived of their property and livelihood after the fact?

If a farm or factory were polluted by former owners, why should the present innocent owner bear the brunt of the problem? Why does the bank or finance agency bear the brunt of clean-up if the borrower fails to do so?

A horse farmer in south central New Jersey told of his curious encounter with the NJDEPE. In order to avoid identification of this case it has been slightly altered. A small stream runs through his property, a stream that horses have used for over one hundred years. It traverses the center of his farm and serves to water some of his stock.

The farmer cut down several trees and moved some boulders in the stream to improve the water flow. He also moved his fence line in one area to permit better access by his horses to the grazing area near the stream as well as to the stream itself.

A disgruntled neighbor called the NJDEPE and an investigator was sent to the scene. The investigator asked a host of questions, took pictures, surveyed the property a few times, and left. He spent about two hours checking the area.

Several weeks later the farmer was called and told that it was "illegal in New Jersey to move rocks in a stream, affect the water flow, cut trees down adjacent to a stream, and/or move a fence as close to a waterway," as he did. All of these seemingly innocent acts have been made illegal because of one environmental rule or another.

The farmer was further told that since no environmental impact statement had been filed, and no approval had been granted by the NJDEPE to perform the acts, there could be a fine or an undescribed penalty for these actions.

The farmer asked, "What corrective measures can I take? I meant no harm." No answer was forthcoming on the phone or in writing. He then wrote two letters seeking advice as to correcting his grievous offense of watering horses. Again, no answer was forthcoming.

Eight months later he received a letter stating that a fine of several thousand dollars per day, calculated from the date the offense occurred, was being considered, all for moving rocks in a waterway, cutting a few trees, watering his horses, and moving a fence line. At the time of publication, the final adjudication is unknown.

A similar but stranger case occurred in a New Jersey municipality. This story was related to the author by a New Jersey state senator who attempted to intervene in the case.

The mayor of a small town in New Jersey took emergency action to assist three homeowners during a heavy rainstorm. The subsequent flooding had endangered the safety of three houses as well as a school sports field. It was determined that several large rocks had been forced together by the torrent of rain that then dammed the stream. Behind the rocks, a line of floating debris had gathered. This confluence caused a blockage that allowed the stream to converge and then overflow.

A homeowner, whose house was being threatened, called the town hall, and the mayor promptly visited the site. The mayor agreed that the homes were threatened, and the softball field was indeed flooding. He quickly assembled a half dozen road department employees as a task force. Equipment was brought in and work started.

In a few hours, the boulders and debris were removed, the rain had ceased, and the emergency was over.

Not quite! Unfortunately, the mayor saved the houses. Another one of Murphy's laws was promptly implemented: "No good deed goes unpunished."

Instead of receiving a nomination for the "small town, quick-acting-mayor-of-the-year award," the official received a visit by a delegation from the NJDEPE. Some erstwhile environmentalist had evidently called, complaining about the town's efforts.

The DEPE inspection, indeed, had revealed that the mayor had reacted improperly. He had entered the stream and performed work on its storm-restricted flow without filing an "Environmental Impact Statement." When it was clearly pointed out that this was an emergency situation, the DEPE pointed out that there is no emergency exemption, and that he had broken the rules. The NJDEPE proposed a $15,000 fine.

The town officials were furious. They called their state senator who agreed with the stupidity of the whole thing and went to bat for his constituents. The best he could do, however, was to assist in getting the penalties reduced. The town finally paid the reduced fine to avoid costly litigation.

But how did the farmer and the mayor get into such difficulty? It really goes back to a vigilante mentality being rekindled by environmentalists. Vigilantism has appeared in American history numerous times, evidently beginning in the 1800s on the frontier. It later spread to more established communities when authority appeared to break down when confronted by lawlessness. Prior to the formation of western style vigilantes, there were groups called "claims associations" that formed to protect the land they had claimed from "claim jumpers" or land speculators.

The height of vigilante justice occurred during the mid-1800s with the most famous incident happening in the San Francisco Bay area. At that time outlaws known as "the Regulators" were suspected of (among many other crimes) having set large and damaging fires that destroyed whole areas.

A group of citizens headed by Sam Brennan caught and hanged one of the gang leaders and several of his cohorts. This San Francisco vigilante group disbanded and reorganized several times over the ensuing five years. It finally disbanded after nearly a decade. Whereas vigilantes of the past operated because of a breakdown of law and order, vigilantes of the present operate *under government sponsorship*. In New Jersey the rebirth of vigilante groups is being aided and abetted by the officials of state government.

In September 1990 Governor Florio announced with biblical fervor: "Let the word go forth to all potential polluters that if they dump on New Jersey they'll be caught . . . bounty provisions have been in place in various environmental statutes, [and] we chose to make them [a] reality."[3]

In the future, 10 percent of the penalties collected, or $250.00 will be paid to citizens who turn in polluters. If the citizen turns in someone who illegally stores hazardous or radioactive waste, the reward is to be higher. It will be set at one-half the penalty collected by the State. "We need seven and a half million pairs of eyes looking for polluters," said Florio.[4]

The State's environmental prosecutor, Steven Madonna, urged all citizens to check boat numbers, car licenses, etc., and report violations to him. The environmental prosecutor has set up special phone numbers, such as, "1-800-NJ-CLEAN," separate reporting systems, and is urging the public interest groups, fishermen, boaters, etc. to organize into platoons.

The same absurd impetus has befallen us, as in the mid-nineteenth century. This time, the vigilantes do not have guns or hanging ropes, but they do have the power to destroy businesses, landowners, farmers, neighbors, and citizens suspected of polluting. No one is immune from this myriad of strange regulations concerning rocks, trees, grass, leaves, air or water. The sad irony is that government regulation has evolved full cycle from that of trained experts, only to revert back to untrained, self-appointed, undirected vigilant citizens. They will begin by observing, then some will climb fences, some will sneak into buildings, and all may cause unpredictable damage to other unsuspecting citizens. So much for search and seizure protections—reasonable doubt, and other constitutional guarantees. Neighbor is set against neighbor—under state auspices.

In June 1991, *The Star Ledger* quoted Environmental Prosecutor Madonna.

"New Jersey citizens should band together to begin monitoring the conditions of the state's rivers so that further contamination can be prevented," a ranking state environmental official said yesterday.

The comments of Steven Madonna, the state's environmental prosecutor, came during a tour of the Passaic River in Kearny. He announced that action had been taken on 15 reports of pollution along the 80-mile length of the waterway brought to the state's attention by the Passaic River Coalition, a watchdog group.[5]

River watchers are becoming active in sighting and reporting spills and discharges of all types. These sightings even permitted the state to go so far as to "order the removal of *graffiti* from a bridge because, Madonna insisted, a river's aesthetics offset the public's impression of the quality of its water.[6]

At the meeting Madonna further proposed many more river watcher groups, soon to be called "patrols" to protect all rivers in New Jersey. It is important to notice the evolution of the new vigilantism—(1) set up phone numbers; (2) get citizens involved; (3) later call them patrols; (4) enroll more groups; then abuses may follow.

Perhaps the groups will get sweatshirts, patrol hats, portable radios, and handbooks. Perhaps they will be asked to inform on their parents. The environment has offered a golden opportunity to power-hungry politicians who are going to save us from the bad guys. The same thought processes have "saved us" before, but they had other names. Unfortunately, hysteria even silences good people during these historical interludes since it becomes very difficult to speak out. It was difficult for honest people to be heard during the Crusades, the Spanish Inquisition, or during similar periods.

The reestablishment of vigilantes will only cease when some extremely active groups crawl into the wrong farmer's shed; or nudge the wrong electric fence, or fall through the wrong loose skylight. Sadly, excess will only return to sanity after the excess proves to be so insane as to cause its reversal.

If our society requires wetlands protection, it should be implemented like all other just laws in a democratic society, not on a vigilante, hysterical, or ex post facto basis.

Nothing could be more ex post facto than the McGown case; as reported in the *Farm Journal:*

> This environmental conflict centers on a 155-acre bottom-land field, part of a 255-acre farm that Rick McGown bought in 1981. "The field, like the rest of the property, had been farmed since the late 1800s," says Rick McGown. It has had drainage tile since the 1940s.
>
> However, brush—mostly Osage orange, honey locust, elm and pin oak—had grown up on many areas since the 1950s after part had been enrolled in the Soil Bank Program, and the owners later moved away. McGown cleared the brush from the farm as time permitted.
>
> In 1987, he set out to repair the levee after the creek broke through. Acting upon a complaint, the Corps of Engineers—in conjunction with the EPA and the U.S. Fish and Wildlife Service—informed McGown he would need a $10 permit to complete the repairs.
>
> "But the permit," says McGown, "was just the beginning." The Corps, he says, wanted him to mitigate the wetland damage he would cause by repairing the levee. That would have involved setting aside some other land. In meetings and correspondence with the Corps, McGown says he attempted to negotiate a solution in good faith that would satisfy both parties.
>
> Ultimately, the Corps showed McGown a proposed permit. Under its "special conditions," he was forbidden to fill

in any low areas or clear any brush inside the levee. Additionally, the area between the levee and the creek also had to be left in timber.

"The levee occupied 6.7 acres. But the Corps wanted me to set aside 25 to 30 acres of timber. That would have given the Corps control of about a quarter of the field," McGown says. "I would pay taxes on it, but I couldn't use it." Also, the special conditions had to be recorded as an encumbrance on the property's title.

During the course of negotiations, the Corps increased its mitigation demand, says McGown—eventually asking to control about a quarter of his entire farm.

McGown believes the amount of land required for mitigation is excessive. "You can't buy a farm, intending to make a living on it, and then just start giving it away," McGown summarizes. "And you can't sell it, either, because the restrictions on its use will make it worth less than what you paid."[7]

Federal and state wetlands legislation not only contain heavy fines, but the possible penalty of going to jail.

No one knows why ECRA, wetlands regulation, and its sisters and brothers have become so punitive. One can rob a bank, mug an elderly woman, or even commit rape, and not face the penalty of an innocent farmer or businessman. In June of 1991 in *Business Week* magazine, Paul Craig Roberts commented on the *emerging nastiness phenomena* as now practiced by the federal government and our bureaucratic agencies:

If the purpose of law is to serve justice, then U.S. law—especially as interpreted by the U.S. government—is failing badly and putting the economy at risk. When the legal consequences of economic activities are virtually imponderable, as they are in the United States today, the economic costs are very high.

Roberts continues by showing how traditional justice and safeguards are being assailed in today's legal climate:

> Plaintiff lawyers and permissive judges have more or less negated the meaning of contracts. Even worse, their success in using novel legal theories to turn claims that were formerly dismissed as nuisances into successful lawsuits has encouraged government attorneys to borrow a sheaf from their book. The main consequence has been a breakdown in the prosecutorial safeguards that traditionally protected the public from an abuse of government power . . . prosecution is not a legitimate method of regulating moral behavior: That's what we have laws for.

The "ECRA thinking," which espouses taking actions against innocent property owners, bystanders, banks, lenders, and uninvolved partners has also infiltrated prosecutorial behavior. Specifically, if one views the Exxon case unemotionally, he will discern gross unfairness inherent in the sad affair; as stated by Paul Craig Roberts in *Business Week:*

> Most outrageous (of recent actions) of all are the government's charges against Exxon Corp. No rational person believes that Exxon intentionally ran its Exxon Valdez supertanker aground in order to discharge refuse matter without a permit and to kill migratory birds without a license. Yet the government's lawsuit implies that it did.[8]

Does one really believe that Exxon's board of directors had a meeting in which they knowingly adopted policies for grounding tankers? Is there not a limit (constitutional or otherwise) for pursuing third parties in these actions? Sadly, if an incident involves the "New Religion," the environment, traditional legal protections seem to melt away. Roberts concludes:

> Determined to criminalize the accident, the government accused Exxon of "willfully and knowingly" employing a captain incapable of keeping the ship off the shoals. The Exxon case is especially troubling because the trumped-up criminal charges are in no way necessary to the civil suit for damages. It is one more example of the government running amok—destroying the law of the land, the safety of its citizens, and the viability of its economy.[9]

Constitutional protections are eroding because the siren song of "The Environment" goes on unopposed. To be against the onslaught of rules, regulations, laws, and penalties makes a protester the same as a polluter. Few can stand publicly against that charge, even though false. But stand we must, or we will all become slaves to runaway environmentalism.

Legislators compete to see who can become *more environmental*. The Pied Piper of Hamelin played an irresistible tune, and we still haven't learned how to stand firm against the sweet sound of this entrapping music.

As Warren T. Brookes reported in *Forbes* magazine in 1989:

> The EPA would become the most powerful government agency on earth, involved in massive levels of economic,

social, scientific and political spending and interference, on a par with the old Energy Department. Don't forget the energy crisis: During the 1970s, a great many less-than-honest scientists confidently predicted the world was about to run out of fossil fuels, and that by 1985, we'd be paying $100 a barrel for oil, or more.

Every year, at least one-sixth of the U.S. is classified by the government's Palmer Index as being in drought. Even though that index overstates the case. All [one] has to do is wait for a warm spell, and capitalize on what mathematicians call noise in the statistics.

Patrick Michaels explains: "We know that the Pacific Ocean current known as El Nino tends to warm and cool in two-year cycles. Just as its warming cycle produced the 1987-88 droughts, in 1989 it cooled sharply, making the United States much cooler and wetter than . . . had been forecast and that is likely to happen in 1990, again. But that means that 1991 and 1992 should be warmer and drier than usual as the El Nino current warms. It won't matter that this has nothing to do with global warming, the media will perceive it that way, and people will tend to believe it."

Bernard Cohen, a physicist at the University of Pittsburgh, warns, in a 1984 book: "Our government's science and technology policy is now guided by uninformed and emotion-driven public opinion rather than by sound scientific advice. Unless solutions can be found to this problem, the United States will enter the 21st century declining in wealth, power and influence . . . The coming debacle is not due to the problems the environmentalists describe, but to the policies they advocate."[10]

Wetlands regulations possess the same economic pitfalls because they were created by the same sister-thinking processes. Environmentalists believe that protection of our water, air, and soil supersedes the legal protection of our citizens. Environmentalists don't say it that way, but that's the way it must be translated. Don't expect protection from the court system. Little stomach or courage exists to protect U.S. citizens when they are pitted against the spotted owl, the camelback salamander, or the great swamp.

Perhaps we can be fined, jailed, or abused, but maybe if we "don't make waves," we can slip our own property through ECRA or Wetlands or their brothers and sisters. That's the normal twentieth century business approach. But don't count on that twentieth century American "wimp" approach to work. America has changed and fairness and justice are less important than vague statements like "societal needs," or "environmental protection."

America was assisted in its economic growth by its transportation system—the transcontinental railway and the interstate highway system, to name two great achievements. Everyone knows that Route 80, which goes from New York City to California, makes a real difference for quick interstate travel. But interstate transportation systems are things of the past.

If one, regardless of his amount of capital, tried to build a high speed rail route or a new interstate highway, he would be totally doomed from the very beginning. The impossible permitting processes, ECRAs, wetlands rules, and their brothers and sisters would halt any attempt at these endeavors.

You could not progress ten miles west of the George Washington Bridge before you encountered the Jersey Meadowlands (home of the N.Y. Giants, who play on filled-in wetlands), which are extensive marshes where cattails still flourish. If the Meadows didn't halt your project, then ECRA would stop you the moment you attempted to traverse the industrial section of Newark.

So, forget the new High Speed Train.

So, forget new Route 80, or its replacement.

Some will say we don't need those things since they are already in place. But wetlands regulations also make it too expensive or nearly impossible to build or replace many bridges, trestles, and filled-in sections of roads or railroad lines.

Some will say that modern transportation is to travel by air. Where are you going to build a new airport requiring one to two thousand acres, a project that doesn't run afoul of environmental concerns?

Where are you going to build a new oil refinery to supply the transportation system? Certainly not in the northeastern United States, where the "not in my backyard" system (NIMBY) exists.

The idea behind regulation should be *to reasonably regulate*. The practical affect of most environmental regulation is that it halts, derails, or causes huge expenses that doom projects. Dooming projects will eventually affect our state and country's infrastructure, economy, and job base. The pendulum must be brought back to the center before this tragedy occurs.

As the definitions, rules, and regulations broaden (that's the only way they will go) we stand to lose more and more. While ECRA is kept within the purviews of manufacturing, processing, or assembling, wetlands is wide open to the imagination of the regulator.

Many areas in the United States are now under attack by the continual expanding of the concept of wetlands. The east and west coasts are covered by broad areas of wetlands, fresh and saltwater. Areas of the North Central and South Central States where swamps, bogs, marshes, lakes, or similar areas exist are also obvious. But other areas are less obvious. Rick Henderson in *The New York Times,* was highly critical of the Army Corps of Engineers for their definition of wetlands.

> Under these new designations "wetlands" now include a North Dakota cornfield where pools of water collect for a week each year during normal spring run-off; a muddy patch between railroad tracks in the center of an Idaho town; irrigation ditches dug by farmers in the West—some of which have been in use since 1900.
>
> Federal agencies have taken supreme advantage of these guidelines. The Environmental Protection Agency started an office of wetlands protection in 1986. Bernard Goode, who ran the Corps' regulatory office from 1981 until 1989, says that the E.P.A. insisted that wetland plants include, in some areas, bluegrass and maples . . .
>
> When the Government deems one's property to be wetlands, the land's value often plummets—sometimes entitling the property owner to compensation under the Fifth Amendment. The Government currently owes landowners more than $1 billion in awards granted by the courts. Since an estimated 80 percent of wetlands are privately owned, further payouts could be staggering.
>
> Consider the New York Borough of Staten Island. To preserve 600 acres of marginal wetlands, taxpayers may have to pay property owners $400 million for their land and install $1 billion in storm drains.[11]

When environmental extremist thinking is applied to issues, the practical human side of the problem is often overlooked. If one wishes to make citizens responsible for actions of others, eventual chaos may result. On July 1, 1991, the

"Clean Water Enforcement Act" became effective. Aside from its impressive title, its ECRA thought process becomes very clear when one learns the facts.

Among other excessively harsh provisions is one that holds licensed operators of publicly owned sewer treatment facilities personally liable for violations of the location's discharge permit. Many engineers and operators are appalled by the consequences of making a few errors since 100 percent compliance on a twenty-four hour per day basis is nearly impossible. These errors can be slight in their overall significance to the water supply, yet can still subject an operator to civil or criminal charges. For example, say a permit allows ten parts per million of a substance, and an average of 50 percent occurs. The 50 percent error, which could subject one to penalties means only that fifteen parts per million were released, instead of ten. This stringency has unnerved sewer plant management. One operator, Peter W. Resota, of Mine Hill, N.J., related this in a letter to the editor of the *Daily Record:*

> Sewerage treatment plants are biological systems that can be upset even under the best of circumstances. Changes in temperature, rainfall, sunlight, and other factors have an effect on the organisms in the treatment process. In addition, operators cannot always control industrial discharge or spills, illegal dumping of wastes into lines, or other unforeseeable excursions. The POTW is also a mechanical operation, involving pumps, motors and highly sophisticated instrumentation. Even the best maintenance program cannot prevent all problems associated with mechanical equipment.
>
> To be held personally liable for these natural, operational, or man-made occurrences beyond our control, which may have an effect on water quality, is unjustified.

The threat of prosecuting sewerage treatment plant operators will only lead to the loss of qualified personnel operating
your wastewater facilities.[12]

It should be obvious that punitive legislation will not solve
pollution problems. This approach will lead to societal breakdown, not improvement.

In a case located in Montague, N.J., the NJDEPE ordered
Nick Frasche to "cease and desist from filling activities
within a freshwater wetland and associated transition area."

In a May 16 notice of violation, the DEPE ordered Frasche
to "cease and desist" from filling activities within a freshwater wetland and associated transition area.

The state said Frasche failed to obtain a freshwater wetlands permit and/or transition area waiver and may have
violated the Freshwater Wetlands Protection Act.

Frasche, interviewed yesterday, insisted the state is still
investigating the matter and will find he does not need a
permit. He said the case involves his operation of a small
farm off New Road. One section of the property is used for
growing Christmas trees, he explained.

Frasche said he read about a new way of growing the trees
by using a thick bed of mulch material around the seedling
pots instead of planting the trees in the ground. He said he
decided to try the method this spring.

"I got the material, made of wood chips and mulch, trucked
in from Pennsylvania," Frasche said. He said he was engaged
in leveling off the 375 cubic yards of material when "apparently somebody reported [he] was filling in wetlands."

Frasche contends he is exempt from the wetlands law
because he has been using the site for agriculture purposes
since 1978. Besides, he said, he was not "filling-in" a wetland.[13]

While the case is still under investigation and no fine has been issued, any chance of growing a crop of trees has been ruined for 1991.

The unbelievable interference in the lives of a free citizenry by these complicated and overbearing regulations is obvious. The power bred by this intrusion is enormous. Busybodies, irate neighbors, overzealous Greens, or the environmental regulators can literally have a field day. They have created a regulatory patchwork that has its own agenda—the total control of citizens lives rather than the protection of the environment.

Protection of the environment cannot be permitted to become a synonym for "deprivation of rights." But that's exactly where we are heading.

The environmental extremists demand that we file "Environmental Impact Statements" to build, develop, enjoy, or improve our property. These statements should include a section that would make two of our founding fathers, Thomas Jefferson and Alexander Hamilton proud. That is: *What is the impact on the owner's constitutional and human rights, what is the cost to him and society; and how does this all fit together?* Unfortunately, environmental impact statements, ECRA applications, and wetlands permits only seek information about water, soil, and air. They do not include sections that inquire about the infringement on the businessman or landowners' rights. Seldom do they balance the rights of employees or the impact on the economic environment. Adverse impact should be judged and based on all the issues relevant, not just the environment. Perhaps this approach would bring the absurdity of it all back to the center. The environmental extremists have never contemplated the words of T. S. Eliot, who said: "Humankind can't stand a strong dose of reality."

X

Conclusion

ECRA must be repealed! Wetland regulation, its sisters and brothers must be curtailed or rewritten. Environmental regulatory thought processes must be returned to time-honored standards of law. Environmental extremism must be pulled back to the regulatory center. Freedom must be restored, fairness must be returned to citizens and businessmen, and laws that penalize the innocent for the good of society are not applicable to a country that espouses democracy.

ECRA must be repealed for many reasons:

It assails the innocent. It creates havoc among businessmen and property owners because of unfair and unjust assignment of clean-up responsibility. The current owner, not the wrongdoer is required to clean up. This produces bizarre results:

Item – If a person owns a property that is now an office building but which once was an industrial site, polluted 100 years ago—he can be totally wiped out financially by previous polluters. *Is he the responsible party?*

Item – If a bank, mortgage company, or leasing company lends money to a company, which fails and goes bankrupt, the *lender* gets ECRA. *Is the lender the responsible party?*

Item – If a tenant moves out in the middle of the night, "stiffs the property owner for the rent," breaks the lease and flees to another jurisdiction, the innocent property *owner* gets ECRA. Did he pollute the site? *Is the owner the responsible party?*

Item– If a company is going through an ECRA case, and its property is being polluted from somewhere else (say, a mile away), the owners are not only stuck with the clean-up, but can be rendered a pauper. They are *victimized* by someone else's pollution and *must prove* it's not their pollution, monitor the pollution, and even clean it up! The person in this case is the victim! *Is the victim the polluter?*

Item– If you own waterfront property polluted by the tides, you may never survive ECRA because the pollutants continually reappear on and beneath your property. You are declared responsible. If your building is built on fill dredged up one hundred years ago, as along the Hudson River, you can't clean it up. NO ONE CAN. ECRA will destroy you and your business for previously legal back filling. *Is the victim in this case the responsible party?*

Item – If a city takes over a distressed property via a tax lien (for unpaid taxes), it must ECRA the property. Older New Jersey cities have hundreds of buildings in this category. None of the cities has the financial ability nor the expertise to ECRA these sites. Hence, many of these properties have been abandoned, and in some cases taken over by the homeless or drug users. *Is the city the responsible party?*

This unfairness has left many New Jersey manufacturers in "shell shock." It is nearly impossible to own, operate, finance, or relocate a manufacturing business in New Jersey. Unless ECRA regulations are rewritten, New Jersey will continue to lose manufacturing jobs at well above the national rate.

The unfair regulatory process creates economic havoc because of the strain of financing one's business. The inability to liquify one's assets creates a desire of many businessmen to move elsewhere. Underlying this allegation is the rapid diminution of manufacturing concerns and manufacturing jobs in New Jersey.

Samuel J. Ehrenhalt, Regional Commissioner of U.S. Labor Statistics said in January 1991:

"What you're seeing really is a devastating story of job losses in key manufacturing industries in New Jersey," Ehrenhalt said.

At 603,000, the total of manufacturing jobs in New Jersey "would be the lowest since 585,000 in 1939," he said.

"The '70s were a bad period for manufacturing, but a clear look at the total picture now shows a lot more weakness in the '80s," the commissioner added. "It's pretty wild: it means that since 1980, New Jersey will have lost 200,000 jobs, substantially above losses in the 1970s, which came to around 100,000 jobs."[1]

In July 1991, the United States Department of Commerce reported economic statistics for the U.S. The New Jersey report was extremely interesting. While the entire United States economy was mired in recession during the reporting period (1st quarter, 1991), the New Jersey results showed a much greater *rate of decline* than the national results.

I believe strongly that this devastation is the result of environmental overregulation and the reputation that is earned by errant policies. Here are the facts as reported by *The Star Ledger* from United States Department of Commerce statistics:

Durable goods manufacturing income in New Jersey fell 3.6 percent, compared with a 2.5 percent decline for the U.S., and nondurable goods manufacturing dropped 1.6 percent compared with an 0.5 percent drop for the nation as a whole.

Personal income in several key sectors of New Jersey's economy fell for the first three months of this year, a sign that the recession deepened throughout the state during that time. . . .[2]

In a similar view:

"The decline from $196.4 billion to $196.1 billion was the first dip in personal income recorded for New Jersey since at least 1982," said Rudolph DePass, regional economist in the Commerce Department's Bureau of Economic Analysis in Washington, D.C.

"It's jolting but it would go along with the job loss," said Rosemary Scanion, chief economist for the Port Authority of New York and New Jersey.[3]

It is quite evident that something other than recession was wrong with the New Jersey economy in 1991. According to newspaper accounts, August of 1991 signaled the twenty-eighth straight month of job market decline. Assistant U.S. Labor Commissioner, Arthur J. O'Neal, said that since February of 1988, 137,000 jobs were lost with 95,500 jobs coming out of the manufacturing sector.

After World War II New Jersey manufacturing jobs had climbed to between 750,000 - 1,000,000. The ascendancy turned into a rapid descent at approximately the same time ECRA and the NJDEPE began its assault on producers and property owners. This rout has continued on a month-by-month basis. "Employment in manufacturing declined over the month by 2,100 jobs to a seasonally adjusted total of 559,800, according to the assistant commissioner."[4]

The figures simply reflect the obvious. From 1969 through 1992, 350,000 manufacturing jobs were lost to the New Jersey economy. The greatest part of these losses occurred in the 1988-1992 period. In 1943 New Jersey was responsible for 5.5 percent of U.S. manufacturing jobs, while in 1992 the same number nose-dived to just 3 percent. When a

government policy is directed at abusing a particular economic sector, then a pullback occurs. Manufacturers are
simply voting with their feet. In many cases (to avoid ECRA
and plant closing laws) businesses simply reduce jobs rather
than close completely. Until enlightened policies are enacted
the economic results of environmental extremism will be
dire.

By September 1991, some signs of recovery were evident
in the National economy. This was not true for New Jersey's
manufacturing sector. Its heavy weight of overregulation and
an anti-business executive branch prompted business to gar-
ner exit visas.

Business bankruptcies in 1991 continued to run at double
the 1990 rate, and manufacturing continued to decline. July
1991 marked the 30th straight month in the New Jersey
manufacturing downturn. The continued economic results
seem to have proven that ten years of anti-manufacturing
policies work as advertised.

ECRA creates a host of problems. We have already seen
how companies cannot be easily sold, merged, or even taken
public under guidelines by the NJDEPE. Delays, extensive
paperwork, and a myriad of excessive measurements have
combined to bring a grinding halt to many New Jersey
business, real estate, and redevelopment transactions. Only
the larger companies with substantial bonding capabilities
can normally move forward on planned mergers.

ECRA reaches into the "deep pockets" of innocent parties—and not necessarily the wrongdoer. The law has created
a host of court cases, economic dislocation, and the "off
balance sheet" liabilities.

In January 1988, the New Jersey Department of Environmental Protection and Energy promulgated its final regula-

tions regarding New Jersey's ECRA statute. The impact of these regulations, difficulties of compliance, complexities, and court challenges, have created problems not foreseen by the backers of this environmental program.

Most businesses or property owners (not residential) in New Jersey are affected by this law, but many do not understand or realize the eventual impact until caught in this web.

ECRA has created many unintended effects: (1) long delays in completing business transactions (1-3 years); (2) use of the New Jersey environmental laws as an anti-takeover device (the company initiating the takeover picks up the environmental responsibilities in New Jersey); (3) reduction in net asset values of process equipment, buildings, etc., which may have *no residual value* because of alleged contamination; (4) inability of subject companies to obtain financing; and (5) perpetuation of current management because ECRA can be triggered by certain changes in management or shareholdings.

Business transactions can't wait for bureaucratic fumbling. Environmental clean-up should be accomplished by other regulatory means, not by hobbling a business deal as it unfolds.

As stated in *"ENR News"*:

> "Jim Sinclair, vice president of the New Jersey Business and Industry Association, noted that in one case, an industrial seller incurred $1 million in penalties from the buyer while waiting for an ECRA approval. The multinational corporate purchaser ultimately built its factory in Singapore.
>
> "It's absolutely insane to put the government in the middle of the transfer of real property," Sinclair says. "If we wanted to invent a policy that's anti-urban, we're doing it here."

ECRA "is wreaking havoc on the industrial real estate market," adds Michael Francois, director of real estate development for the New Jersey Economic Development Authority. "Only its status as a state agency allowed the authority to expedite ECRA approval for part of the $500 million development of the former Campbell Soup Company manufacturing site along the Camden waterfront," he admits.

"That approval took only a few months from the completion of the site study—a record in DEPE," says Francois. "It normally takes that long just to get a case manager assigned."[5]

ECRA just doesn't perform as advertised. Ask the man who purchased a site in Essex County, N.J., for approximately $1,200,000. The site had previously *gone through two ECRA filings* successfully. The new buyer relied on the previous filings and felt protected by a "buyer insurance law." But after he substantially renovated the property, he again put it up for sale and, because of a change in use, had to file a third ECRA (in four years). He originally felt it would be a "cakewalk," since the property had already passed twice. A well drilled in a different location at the request of a new case manager detected hitherto unseen underground contamination. The new owner was irate. He claimed that the contamination had come from off site. But he had to prove his claim. His consultant told him it could take at least a year and cost several hundred thousand dollars. The case may go to court and is at this writing unresolved.

If each site is to be as clean as a hospital floor with everything measured in parts per billion, how and where is business to be conducted? We all agree that no one has the right to pollute. But some use of the earth's surface is required for man to exist and manufacture his goods.

Is there a solution? An editorial in the McGraw-Hill *Construction Weekly* suggests an answer.

> Certainly identifying toxins on a site is beneficial to the public and fair to a potential buyer. But the issue in New Jersey is the extent to which the Department of Environmental Protection and Energy places itself in the middle of a private transaction. Any foul material must be cleaned up eventually, but that is no reason to quash an imminent industrial project.
>
> That is not to say, "Let the buyer beware." Let the buyer, the state and the public be informed. Then permit a private arrangement to take its course with the parties reaching an agreement on liability for cleaning up whatever mess exists.[6]

Indeed, the State of Illinois picked the route of reporting to the regulators but not standing in the middle of transactions and abusing all parties. In adopting its property transfer law the State of Illinois chose to keep government informed, but "out of the business process."

Environmental protection has become a form of mind control because we blindly believe what we are told. Soon you believe you are doing something wrong if someone says it long enough! In New Jersey we are told that the removal of leaves and grass clippings can be hazardous. A bonfire is illegal. We are told that a fire company conducting a drill that uses a real fire is illegal. But the same fire company conducting the same drill at an *approved* drill site is okay. Move rocks in a stream and you can be fined (or even jailed) for violating river flow without an environmental impact statement on file or a permit. Unclogging a stream without filling out an environmental impact statement is totally illegal, even though the action could prevent flooding. Pesticides are legal on food but not in the soil of a business site!

There are hundreds of crisscross regulations. You must by the very nature of things run afoul of one or more of them. If you store wood for a period of time, you can be cited as a possessor of waste without a permit. If you take down trees near a stream on your own property, you can be fined even if you are a farmer.

In New Jersey, the state government has now established an environmental prosecutor. The position seems above criticism because protection of the air and water is like virginity. But this job by its very nature creates its own inanity. In the story related below Steven Madonna, New Jersey's Environmental Prosecutor, succeeded in fining a landowner $8,700 *for storing dirt!* In doing so he stated that he would diligently look for other transgressors of the same "dirt storing" persuasion. There was no claim that the stored dirt polluted the environment, contained oil, or was unclean in any way. It was just dirt. The crime—it was stored too close to a river. The dirt could get into the river.

But earth storage, like wood storage, can be illegal if it's not piled in accordance with environmental regulations. There are regulations of almost every kind that can enforce *any position* that the regulators wish to take. This particular *illegal storage of earth* occurred in May 1991, near the Pequanock River in Northern New Jersey. A road and sewer contractor was hired to excavate earth near Riverdale Borough to complete work for the town. He needed a temporary place to store the clean fill while he was completing the project.

A friend offered him his property for the storage, and numerous truckloads of earth were placed there. The NJDEPE discovered this aboveground earth storage and found it to be a "gross violation." It was stored too close to a river.

The landowner said he followed the directive, paying $6,000 to remove the dirt, and added the State Department of Environmental Protection and Energy (DEPE) also fined him $8,700.

DEPE officials said the amount is a settlement offer, explaining that it was a percentage of the maximum $40,000 they could have fined [him.] Madonna said that since the fill was taken out so quickly, he considered the matter closed.[7]

The owner paid the fine even though he "thought he was doing the contractor and town a favor"—a favor which cost him almost $15,000. The owner further stated that he was donating part of his property as a right of way during the road-widening process and did not think he did anything wrong.

Storage of dirt a crime? It was because the regulators found a specific regulation it violated. Lest you believe this was a bureaucratic aberration or perversity, think again. The State Environmental Prosecutor Steven Madonna said, "It's like the State Police stopping a speeder on the Garden State Parkway; we can't get all of them, but we are going to be looking more in that area." (The "area" that Madonna is referring to was "storage of dirt.")[8]

Dirt, wood, grass, leaf, and earth storers, beware, you are not safe in New Jersey. Mind control does strange things. If you believe that protection of the environment transcends everything else, then anything done in its name is acceptable. People with these beliefs don't care about the rule of law, private property rights, the U.S. Constitution, due process, the democratic process, or even about people. To staunch environmentalists, liberty is an abstraction and protection of their favorite cause transcends legal protections. Petty despots abound in history; unfortunately, today's despots have caught the nation's ear.

A New Jersey inventor and businessman, Frank Reick, put it this way:

> There is a very serious question that should be raised about ECRA. How did a law that was basically well-intended turn into such a disaster? The fault lies squarely on the doorstep of the state legislature.
>
> They passed an idea and made it law. They then gave a group of bureaucrats carte blanche to write the law, set standards, write rules and then interpret it's own standards and rules to suit itself. It was funded by penalties assessed on those it ensnared in the resulting web of arbitrariness.
>
> That's the legislative equivalent of giving Jesse James the keys to the bank and telling him to guard it.
>
> I've spent the better part of a year listening to horror stories from innocent people whose lives were destroyed, savings wiped out and business expansion plans halted. They tell stories of terror and fear of retribution if they speak out against the bureaucratic outrages that are committed against them. Many have been warned by their lawyers to keep quiet. Many, who are able, are planning to take their businesses to a different state!
>
> I can only hope that now these people who were previously intimidated will step out, exercise their First Amendment rights and tell their stories for the historical record. They have a moral responsibility to do so.
>
> Perhaps then when society hears of the outrages that have been committed under the guise of cleaning up the environment, the legislature will mend its ways and never, never again, give a legislative blank check to a bureaucrat.
>
> Just as the captain of a ship must be held responsible for hitting an iceberg, the administration and storm troopers of ECRA must be held accountable for the devastation they have caused.

The legislators must see that the mindless zealots who would hold innocent people guilty of environmental crimes they did not commit are held accountable for their actions.

The beneficiaries of the ECRA laws have largely been the bureaucrats, self-appointed consultants and attorneys. They skim our state's resources off the top before taxes. These are funds removed from productive activity. All society suffers.

A sensible law would be one that had well-defined standards set by responsible members of the community based on scientific fact and historical realities. A law that encourages cooperation between individuals, businesses and government to reach our common goal of a better environment is what we need . . . not a Frankenstein monster![9]

Now that the environmental protection process has invaded our psyche, sanity, liberty, jobs, economy, and way of life, it must be brought back to the middle. The ECRA virus, with its brother and sister diseases must be turned back. Sanity must be restored to environmental protection.

Transgressions or crimes must be treated similarly. Why is throwing a bottle in the ocean a $25,000 fine, but stealing a purse, or a (first offense) street mugging, only a suspended sentence?

Recall how ECRA punishes innocent parties. Joint and several liability, where an absentee landlord inherits a tenant's problem or a previous owner's or tenant's problem is punishing the innocent party. The words "without regard to fault" imply deep pockets and no regard for *innocence* or *guilt*. If drums were buried fifty years ago and the current owner, bank, lessee, or lessor discovers them in the course of ECRA— is the discoverer the innocent or guilty party? The DEPE, as well as Governor Kean, has stated: "that although ECRA does require the current owner or operator to clean up the site, this does not preclude that party from pursuing legal actions for cost recovery through the courts" (Governor Thomas H. Kean's letter of June 9, 1988). But this just isn't a practical answer! A person is guilty in ECRA by *mere possession* of property or a business, not by guilt or wrongdoing.

The government argued its case. Richard T. Dewling, Commissioner of the NJDEPE, sent a letter to Assemblyman Garabed Haytian as follows:

> ECRA does not "punish" the innocent. Both a landlord and tenant are jointly and severally liable under ECRA. It was, after all, clearly the intent of the legislation to provide for timely remediation of environmental problems by the current owner/operator of an industrial establishment. This was due to our experience of long litigation delays to have contaminated sites remediated.[10]

If a tenant illegally stores hazardous wastes or errs under ECRA, it is okay to attack the landlord "due to our . . . long litigation delays to have contaminated sites remediated." The issues for the officials seem to be: (1) bureaucratic convenience; (2) prompt remediation; (3) the intent of the statute as interpreted by the bureaucrat.

Why aren't these issues addressed: who's guilty, what's fair, and what's just? The excuse to void our liberty is long litigation delays, causing bureaucratic inconvenience.

In "Trashing the Planet," the authors Dixie Lee Ray and Lou Guzzo, state the following intelligent approach to environmental overkill:

> First, a person can put pressure, individually and through groups, on members of the legislative branch, both state and

federal, to refrain from acting precipitously on expensive "cures" for unproven environmental ills. Ask for evidence. It's public tax money that they are proposing to spend; it should not be wasted.

Second, don't succumb to the argument put forward by political environmentalists that action must be taken in advance of understanding the problem, "just in case." Keep in mind that they have a job or position to protect. Remember, the alarmists depend on continued crises, even if they are contrived, to keep themselves in business. Insist on facts.

Third, keep a sense of perspective. This old earth has been through a lot, including drastic climate changes, without any help from humans. It will continue to change. The earth has never been stable or remained the same for long.

Finally, humans cannot live on earth without altering it and without using natural resources. Our responsibility is to be good stewards of the environment and to remember that a well-tended garden is better than a neglected wood lot. It is demeaning beyond belief to consider mankind simply another species of animal, no better and no worse than wild beasts.

We human beings are what we are—imperfect but well-meaning and capable of improvement. We learn from mistakes. We have the ability to think rationally and we should do so more often. We also have the gift to make conscious choices; and we should choose to purchase knowledge and understanding that will better the lot of all species on the planet.[11]

Perhaps the reason why ECRA and its brothers and sisters should be expelled from the scene is now clear. There is little difference in the implementation of environmental tyranny from any other kind—the latter just has a better ring to it.

The solution to curing overzealous environmental enforcement of property transfers is relatively simple. In the United States we have been using the concept for nearly sixty years. In the "Securities and Exchange Act," used in the transfer of negotiable securities (which is a form of property), requirements exist regarding the valid concept of disclosure, documentation, and notice. The seller of securities is required to provide the buyer with a prospectus, which includes financial statements and full disclosure about securities that are being transferred. The prospectus must accurately tell about a company, its history, business, employment, earnings, balance sheet, and so on. A copy is filed with the SEC that then reviews it and permits (or halts) the sale of the common stock, bonds, or warrants.

If the transfer of property were handled this way (as it is substantially done in Illinois), then many of the problems with the ECRA thought process and its unwarranted intrusion into citizens' lives could be solved. The Illinois law, patterned after security law disclosure, works as follows:

ILLINOIS RESPONSIBLE PROPERTY TRANSFER ACT (IRPTA)

Who must report?

1. Party to real property transfer which:
   a. contains one or more facilities which are subject to reporting under Section 312 of the federal Emergency Planning and Community Right-to-Know Act of 1986.
   b. has underground storage tanks which require notification under Section 9002 of the Solid Waste Disposal Act.

2. Parties to transfer include:
   a. Seller, grantor, mortgagor, or lessor.
   b. Buyer, trustee under a trust deed, mortgagee, grantee, or lessee.

What is the procedure?

1. Transferor must submit a disclosure document to transferee within 30 days following signing of contract or 30 days before transfer.

2. Disclosure document to indicate "environmental defects," a hazardous material-related activity.

3. Transferee may void contract if disclosure document reveals any unknown defects.

4. Within 30 days after transfer, both parties are responsible for filing copies of disclosure document with county recorder and the IEPA, Division of Land Pollution Control.

When did the legislation take effect?

It applied to transactions that occurred after January 1, 1990.[12]

The Illinois law represented an informed, studied approach and was specifically designed not to duplicate the horrors of New Jersey's failure. It mandates the providing of information to banks, mortgage companies, as well as buyers so that everyone plays on a level playing field. A property can be evaluated and a business deal accomplished with clean-up in mind. However, this approach to clean-up doesn't destroy people's lives, businesses, or transactions. Clean-up can be handled over time, and negotiated by banks, buyers and sellers.

Again, the key to the Illinois (IRPTA) Responsible Property Transfer Act is disclosure. The prospectus must be handed over to the purchaser, bank, and/or state agency, thirty days from the signing of the contract. If the prospectus is false or misleading, then the lease, rental agreement, or purchase contract can be legally terminated. Violations carry penalties of $1,000 per day, or if the violation is part of a proven fraudulent transfer, the penalty can be $10,000 per day.

This disclosure approach is sensible, respectful of constitutional guarantees, and workable. It keeps bureaucrats out of the business process, yet the state is informed about property pollution and agreements regarding clean-ups. A large environmental bureaucracy becomes unnecessary, since it becomes solely a receiving, reviewing, and enforcement agency. Most importantly it utilizes free market economic forces to do the job, and does not seek taxpayer funding.

Even though IRPTA does not put companies through an ECRA-like meat grinder, its approach will work. In today's world, who would knowingly purchase a polluted property? Purchasers and sellers will work out acceptable clean-ups, and raise or lower purchase prices accordingly. In the long run this method will work because it respects the forces of the market place by information, knowledge, and disclosure. It will eliminate the unfairness, coercion, and extortionary processes found in the "ECRA Virus."

It is my judgement that the Illinois process will work and work well. The ECRA method has failed, will continue to fail since it breeds injustice, and destroys economic viability.

If land transfers were handled like security transfers, then many practical problems could be resolved. There would be few delays. Banks could help to finance both companies and clean-up because they would once again be only lenders and not have secondary liability.

Raising capital could proceed normally as the seller could outline his remediation and still raise funds to solve the problems. Owners of old properties could sell to stronger hands; for example, a developer could agree to clean up the site and deduct an amount from the sale price or the required funds borrowed from a mortgage company.

Inner cities could be redeveloped since the town itself would not be a party to the remediation problems.

Tenants should be responsible for their own clean-up; landlords would be out of the loop. If a landlord caused a problem, he should be responsible. If he didn't, then the person who caused it should remedy the situation.

Dr. Jo Kwong, in her book *Myths About Environmental Policy,* concludes with the following straightforward approach:

> Much of the conventional wisdom about environmental policy falls short because it relies on government solutions and fails to recognize the link between private enterprise and environmental well-being. Over the last century, economic growth and technological development have enabled Americans to produce cleaner water, more sanitary and efficient waste disposal, more forests, and a safer, more plentiful food supply.
>
> Free enterprise has also contributed to environmental consciousness. Prosperity affords us the opportunity and resources to focus on environmental concerns. In developing nations, where populations struggle to survive, food and shelter come first, long before environmental quality.

Still, there are important environmental concerns that Americans need to address. Some stem from the lack of identifiable property rights. Where property rights are absent, as with many air and water resources, abuse and degradation [are] typically the result. Other problems arise out of political dealings and government mismanagement of resources. Still others are simply created by the stresses from human civilization.

Fortunately, we can overcome these challenges with rational policies and scientific advances. The free enterprise system provides our strongest and most efficient tool. Indeed, history has proven it to be the best system for managing our resources and providing technology. Future environmental policies must rely less on government solutions and more on private enterprise, building upon the natural link between economic and ecologic development.[13]

The New Jersey *Law Journal,* in an editorial entitled "The New Religion," put it this way:

For the past 20 years or so the protection of the environment has taken on many of the attributes of a religion. Its adherents, the environmentalists, have aligned themselves against the purported forces of darkness and evil. Those who question the faith are castigated and ridiculed as heretics and worse—the very despoilers of mother earth.

Nowhere has this passion play run as long and as consistently as in New Jersey. And we would be remiss if we failed to recognize that which is popular is also politically expedient. Our candidates for elective office have tripped over themselves extolling their environmental records and trumpeting the strength of their commitment.

In analyzing the relationship between economic prosperity and protection of the environment, it is possible to lose sight of the need for balance and moderation. It is with this in mind that we considered a recent report by the state Labor Department indicating that during a 28-month period, the state lost almost 200,000 jobs. These included 95,500 in the manufacturing sector, 43,200 in trade and 41,000 in construction. Some of these statistics can certainly be attributed to national, or at least regional, trends. But it would be myopic to ignore the contributing factors that are peculiar to New Jersey.

We can only wonder what type of signal the state government is sending to New Jersey's businesses and industries, when the Department of Environmental Protection and Energy assesses more than $130 million in monetary penalties in a 12-month period and promises to run its programs from this "source of revenue" in the future. Are not the governor and his environmental prosecutor encouraging the exodus and the disinvestment by their threats of prison terms for those who run afoul of the state's myriad requirements? Glitzy and expensive media campaigns may influence the electorate but decision-makers in the business community are more interested in the government's actions than in what it says in paid advertisements. In light of the hostile business climate that has been created, given the choices, the results are not surprising.

We are certainly not suggesting that the state abandon important environmental objectives. However, after two decades of almost blind adherence to green orthodoxy, a modicum of maturity and sophistication is now necessary in addressing environmental issues. To avoid even more severe consequences, these issues need to be placed in an appropriate context. This will require a number of measures such as lowering and redirecting the rhetoric, streamlining procedural requirements, recognizing that certain activities are so minor that they do not need to be regulated and establishing a more temperate approach concerning enforcement. While some of the extreme environmentalists are bound to be displeased, at least their spouses and children may have the opportunity to find employment and housing in New Jersey.[14]

Our society cannot stand as liberty loving and democratic when those who spread fear in the name of righteousness are allowed to preach their false religion unchallenged.

Appendix 1

Summary of Decision, May 6, 1991
Appellate Division of Superior Court of New Jersey

Re: ECRA Regulations

On May 6, 1991, the Appellate Division of the Superior Court of New Jersey issued its opinion in the consolidated challenges by industry and environmental groups to a number of the regulations passed pursuant to the Environmental Clean-up Responsibility Act ("ECRA or "the ACT"), in re Adoption of N.J.A.C. 7:26B (Docket Nos. A-2403-87T1, A-2521-87T1, A-2522-87T1, A-2523-87T1, A-2524-87T1 and A-364-89T3). As you are aware, ECRA imposes investigation and remediation responsibilities on owners and operators of industrial establishments as a precondition for the sale, transfer, or termination of operations at these facilities.

The industry appellants attacked portions of the regulations which (1) provide that certain transactions involving a parent corporation trigger ECRA obligations with respect to an industrial establishment owned or operated by a subsidiary of the parent; (2) define the statutory ECRA trigger of a "proceeding through which an establishment becomes nonoperational for health or safety reasons" as including temporary closings for fires, explosions or other events; (3) apply ECRA to some situations where only a portion of the real property of the establishment is conveyed; and (4) define such terms as "sale of the controlling share of the assets" of a corporation, which is a statutory ECRA trigger.

Those appellants also attacked the regulations which provide that ECRA is applicable to any sale of a general partnership interest, as well as to certain sales of limited partnership interests in a partnership which operates an industrial establishment. In addition, the appellants challenged the validity of the regulations which define "clean-up plan" to include measures for remedying contamination not actually on the site of the industrial establishment. It is this aspect of the decision, concerning contamination which has migrated off the site of the industrial establishment, which has been the focus of the recent media attention. In brief, the Court ruled that pursuant to ECRA, the NJDEP may not require, as part of the clean-up plan, procedures for remedying contamination from an industrial establishment which exists off-site, on properties not owned by the operator of the establishment subject to ECRA. The rationale for this portion of the decision will be discussed in greater detail below.

The central points of the ruling are presented in the order they appear in the decision.

I. Parent-Subsidiary Triggers

The first substantive question that was presented to the Court was whether the regulations impermissibly expand ECRA by imposing clean-up responsibility because of changes in a parent corporation which owns an industrial subsidiary. Specifically, the appellants challenged those portions of NJDEP regulations which provide that ECRA is triggered by sales, transfers, or dissolutions of the parent corporation which owns or operates a subsidiary which, in turn, owns or operates an industrial establishment. The attack was directed to the basic principle that a change at the parent corporation level might trigger ECRA, as well as to the implementing, regulatory definition of "controlling interest" in N.J.A.C. 7:26B-1.3.

The Court ruled that despite the appellants' contention that the parent-subsidiary regulation went beyond the authority of the ECRA statute, the statute was nevertheless broad and inclusive enough to encompass, within the term "change in ownership," events not normally construed as such. According to the Court, the specification in the statute that the term "change in ownership" "includes but is not limited to" certain enumerated events, suggests that NJDEP could reasonably determine that other types of transactions might constitute a "change in ownership" for ECRA purposes. Consequently, the Court concluded that the statute does authorize the regulations in question because it, in effect, defines "change of ownership" to include events which could affect a corporation's financial ability to clean up hazardous waste and does not limit the term to the transfer of the actual physical plant. Moreover, the Court interpreted ECRA as implicitly authorizing the NJDEP to determine what transactions, in addition to those listed in the statute, should constitute a subject change in ownership. Thus, the Court ruled against the appellants with regard to their attack on the parent-subsidiary trigger issue.

II. Regulation Defining "Corporate Reorganization"

The next question presented by the appellants was whether the regulatory definition of "corporate reorganization not substantially affecting the ownership of the industrial establishment," impermissibly narrows the statutory exclusion from ECRA. N.J.S.A. 13:1k-8b provides that a "corporate reorganization not substantially affecting the ownership of the industrial establishment" is not a change in ownership which triggers ECRA. The implementing regulations for this provision, included in the "Definitions" section of N.J.A.C. 7:26B-1.3, define this phrase, in pertinent part, as "the restructuring or reincorporation by the board of directors or the shareholders of a corporation, which does not diminish the availability of the assets for any environmental clean-up, or diminish the Department's ability to reach the assets. . . ."

The appellants contended that there was no statutory basis for the requirement that there be no diminution in the assets available for environmental clean-up and no reduction in NJDEP's ability to reach those assets. They claimed that the statute required only that the corporate reorganization not substantially affect ownership and that it did not impose any financial criteria on the reorganization. In addition, the appellants maintained that the regulation is so broad that is it unclear what criteria a corporation must satisfy in order to fall within the exemption.

The Court agreed with the NJDEP's contention that the regulation was consistent with the statute. The Court stated that the statutory definition of "change in ownership" is broad enough to include financial changes and not simply changes which occur with transfer of shares of stock or transfer of a physical plant. Indeed, the Court concluded that it appears "necessary" to define a "corporate reorganization not substantially affecting ownership" as one which does not entail significant changes in the financial ability of a corporation to comply with ECRA.

III. Regulation Defining "Controlling Interest"

The third issue presented by the appellants revolved around the definition of "controlling interest" in N.J.A.C. 7:26B-1.3. "Controlling interest" is presently defined as the interest held by an individual or individuals owning more than 50% of the stock or the interest held by an individual or individuals who own less than 50% of the stock but who possess the power to "direct or cause the direction of the management and policies of a corporation." The appellants argued that the regulation does not specify what types of stock, preferred or common, are to be included in determining controlling interest transfers and whether it is 50% of the value of the stock or the physical number of shares which triggers the Act. They also contended that it is contrary to general corporate law to trigger ECRA where there is a sale by a group of persons which owns less than 50% of the stock of the corporation but which indirectly or directly has the power to direct or cause the direction of the management policies of the corporation to change. Finally, the appellants maintained that no individual shareholder, as a shareholder, would ever possess such power.

The Court found it reasonable to use the sale of more than 50% of the stock of a corporation as a "bright line test." The Court also noted that the failure to specify the precise type or class of stock (common, preferred, etc.), does not render the regulation ambiguous. Finally, the Court found no confusion in the regulation simply because the regulation does not suggest when the 50% test is to be applied. The Court noted that if the regulation does not require aggregation of sales over a specific time period, then the 50% trigger must logically be read as applying to block sales in that amount, not staged or incremental sales.

The Court also rejected the appellants' challenge to that portion of the regulation triggering ECRA when there is a sale of less than 50% of the stock by the person or persons who have the power, directly or indirectly, to manage the policies of the corporation. The Court noted that fewer than a majority of the shareholders of a corporation could effectively exercise control through the officers and board of directors. The Court also found that a shareholder may not have direct authority to influence the policies of a corporation but may nonetheless have indirect power to do so.

IV. Regulation Defining "Cessation of All Operations"

The next issue raised was whether the NJDEP's regulatory definition of "cessation of operations" as including "substantially all" operations is inconsistent with the statute. The appellants contended that there is no basis for using the concept "substantially all" operations when the statute itself refers to a cessation of "all" operations.

The Court ruled that N.J.A.C. 7:26B-1.9, with standards, would allow a company to demonstrate without much inconvenience that a discontinuance of one minor sub-operation, (even if this discontinuance fails the 90% test) should not trigger ECRA. (The Court's emphasis on the need to express standards for nonapplicability decisions is discussed in greater detail below.) The Court noted that, by providing a "bright line" 90% reduction test governing when a business must either comply with ECRA or seek a determination of nonapplicability, the regulation at issue was not onerous or problematic.

The Court explained, however, with regard to this challenge as well as the challenges to parent-subsidiary triggers, corporate reorganizations and transfers of "controlling interest," that it was rejecting the appellants' challenges, subject to a recasting by the NJDEP of reasonable standards for the determination of nonapplicability.

V. Standards for Nonapplicability

The Court held that the regulations challenged by the appellants, as discussed herein, can be upheld only if the NJDEP develops and promulgates reasonable standards for nonapplicability in N.J.A.C. 7:26B-1.9, so that the regulated community has some guidance for conduct and the NJDEP has some structure for the exercise of its discretion.

While the Appellate Division did not make any precise recommendations as to the content of these standards, it suggested that the NJDEP "might well want to articulate a desire to exempt entities or transactions where "triggering" activity would not result in any material changes in New Jersey operations, would not weaken the ability of a company to ultimately comply with ECRA or other environmental mandates, or would be so formalistic as to have utterly no consequence relevant to the Act." The Court suggested the standards should also include a reasonable time limit for the NJDEP to act on any application for nonapplicability.

The Court remanded this issue to the NJDEP to draft and promulgate specific standards for the application of N.J.A.C. 7:26B-1.9 within ninety days, stating that this "safety-valve" section is critical to the survival of the portions of the regulations challenged by the appellants, but, at least temporarily, is upheld by the Court in this decision.

VI. Closures for Health or Safety Reasons

The appellants challenged the regulatory definition of that section of the statute defining "closing, terminating or transferring operations" (N.J.S.A. 13:1K-8b) as including transactions or proceedings through which an industrial establishment becomes nonoperational for health or safety reasons. The Court concurred with appellants' analysis that, in reading the definition of N.J.S.A. 13:1k-8b as a whole, the phrase "any other transaction or proceeding through which an industrial establishment becomes nonoperational for health or safety reasons or undergoes change in ownership" means that the statute applies to a "proceeding" in which an industrial establishment becomes nonoperational or a "transaction" through which it undergoes a change in ownership. The Court struck down the regulatory language which included the phrase "including but not limited to explosions, fires, or other similar events." The Court reasoned that while a fire or explosion may well be the cause of closing a facility for health or safety reasons, it was the official determination of closure, which might be based on such an event, which the Legislature intended to trigger ECRA. The Court also noted that the definition of "closing" included a "temporary" closing for a period of not less than two years. (N.J.S.A. 13:1K-8b, N.J.A.C. 7:26B-1.5(b)(14).) Temporary closings, therefore which extended for two years or more would trigger ECRA, while other closings for a lesser period would not. Moreover, the Court stated that closures for health and safety reasons, as referred to in the statute, were intended to encompass closures for a period of less than two years, ordered by a court or regulatory agency but which were not otherwise subject to ECRA.

VII. Sales of Partnership Interests as Triggers

The Court ruled that the NJDEP should administratively rectify the failure of N.J.A.C. 7:26B-1.5(b)(10) to allow an entity to demonstrate, pursuant to the nonapplicability section, that ECRA should not apply to particular transfers of partnership interests. The Court ruled that this omission in the regulation concerning partnerships renders the regulation arbitrary and unreasonable since it does not permit recourse to the nonapplicability review.

Ultimately, the Court held that the partnership provisions of the regulations are invalid because the NJDEP did not demonstrate why the Legislative policies underlying ECRA require that the statute should always be triggered by the sale of a partnership interest, an event which is not specifically included as a statutory trigger. The Court noted that the rationale for the regulation is also drawn into question by the fact that other parts of the regulations allow a corporation, by recourse to the nonapplicability provision, to demonstrate that certain events, although specifically described by the statute as ECRA triggers, should not, in particular circumstances, be viewed as such.

VIII. Changes in SIC Industry Number Triggers

The appellants also attacked the second paragraph of N.J.A.C. 7:26B-1.3 which includes in the definition of "closing, terminating, or transferring operations," any changes in operations sufficient to change the primary Standard Industrial Classification ("SIC") Industry Number of an establishment from one which is subject to the Act to one which is not subject to the Act. The Court rejected this attack on the grounds that if there is a change in manufacturing operations sufficient to trigger a change in the SIC Industry Number, then there has been a cessation of the activity which caused a facility to be considered an industrial establishment in the first place. The Court found that it is reasonable to consider ECRA triggered when there is a shift in the primary operations which brought the facility within the ambit of the Act in the first place.

IX. Regulation Defining Sale of Controlling Share of Assets

The next issue raised by the appellants was whether the regulatory definition of "sale of controlling share of assets" impermissibly exceeds the statutory definition. N.J.S.A. 13:1k-8b defines "closing, terminating or transferring operations" to include a "sale of the controlling share of the assets of an industrial establishment." The appellants claimed that the Legislature intended to trigger the statute only when there was a sale of "all or substantially all" of the assets of an industrial establishment not made in the ordinary course of business.

The Court rejected this and other related contentions of the appellants by saying that "controlling share of the assets," by its plain terms, means something other than "substantially all" assets. The Court also stated that a business is permitted to demonstrate that ECRA is not appropriately triggered and is inapplicable, even if it would be deemed, by a literal reading of the regulations, to have sold the controlling share of its assets. (N.J.A.C. 7:26B-1.5(6)(3), incorporating N.J.A.C. 7:26B-1.9.)

X. ECRA as Site Specific

Perhaps most significantly, the Court upheld the appellants' contention that ECRA obligates an owner of an industrial establishment to clean up only the site of the business operations and that ECRA has no application to discharges on-site which may flow off-site.

The Court stressed that N.J.S.A. 13:1k-8 uses language which specifically refers to a clean-up plan of hazardous substances and wastes that remain on the premises. In addition, the Court pointed out that "negative declaration" is defined as a statement, approved by the NJDEP, that there has been no discharge of hazardous substances or wastes on the site, or that there remain no hazardous substances or wastes at the site of the industrial establishment.

The Court conceded that one could reasonably argue that the purpose of ECRA is undermined if owners are allowed to transfer sites without cleaning up discharges which have flowed onto areas surrounding the site. However, the Court affirmed the legal axiom that, when a statute speaks plainly, courts will enforce it as written. In addition, the Court explained that, while ECRA is a remedial statute which is ordinarily liberally or generously construed to effectuate its purpose, the courts, when interpreting other remedial environmental statutes, have narrowly construed statutory language which imposes liability on a landowner. Consequently, whatever the policy reasons in support of requiring the owner of an industrial establishment to clean up contamination on and off the site before transferring the property, the Court found that the regulation, as interpreted by the NJDEP, goes beyond the express terms of the statute since the statute speaks only in terms of hazardous substances remaining on the site.

The Court noted the State's power under the Spill Compensation and Control Act to compel a property owner to remedy any discharge onto land which threatens the natural resources of the State, even if it overflows the property boundary. It opined, however, that this power cannot be read into ECRA, by fiat of the NJDEP, so as to require an industrial establishment to conduct an off-site clean-up as a condition to a sale. Consequently, the Court found that the portion of N.J.A.C. 7:26B-1.3, which requires that a clean-up plan include procedures for remedying off-site contamination from an industrial establishment on properties not owned by the operator of the establishment, is beyond the scope of the ECRA-enabling legislation, and is invalid.

We believe, therefore, that it may be argued, as a logical corollary to this portion of the ruling, that if there is no enforceable off-site clean-up requirement under ECRA, then the NJDEP also cannot require an investigation of off-site contamination.

XI. The Physical Extent of "Industrial Establishment"

The appellants presented a challenge to the NJDEP's definition of the physical extent of an "industrial establishment" and maintained, in that connection, that the statute does not refer to "lots or blocks" on which a business is conducted. The Court interpreted the argument to be that the statute covers only the area on which the business is actually operated, excluding those areas on the same "lot" which are not used for the business. In this connection, the appellants also argued that there is no authority for the NJDEP to include contiguous vacant land as part of an industrial establishment.

The Court rejected these contentions and defined the term "industrial establishment" as including not only the lot, as defined for tax or deed purposes, on which the pertinent facility is located, but also the contiguous parcels used in conjunction with the business, as well as contiguous parcels of vacant land controlled by the owner or operator of the facility.

XII. Intrafamily Transfers and Condemnation as Triggers

Another issue presented by the appellants concerned the exemption for intrafamily transfers. This contention, raised by the environmental group appellants, stated that the statute provides no authorization for this exemption. The Court ultimately sustained this regulatory exemption, deferring to the NJDEP's judgment that intrafamily transfers do not need to be regulated by ECRA.

With regard to the appellants' challenge of the NJDEP's regulation requiring ECRA compliance in the case of partial condemnations of industrial establishments, the Court held that the NJDEP's regulation applying ECRA to condemnations, partial or otherwise, is eminently reasonable and sustainable. The Court noted that the Act applies to a change in ownership (N.J.S.A. 13:1k-8(b) and condemnation does result in a change in ownership. It also reasoned that the concern that hazardous substances be cleaned up when an industrial establishment ceases operations is perhaps more compelling when the transferee is a public body than when an industrial establishment is transferred to a private entity, since the public entity may have lesser resources with which to correct environmental problems. The Court concluded that it would be inequitable to permit a landowner to avoid ECRA compliance by the "fortuitous event" of condemnation.

As to the appellants' contention that it is unreasonable and beyond the scope of the ECRA statute to require compliance when there is only a partial condemnation and an industrial establishment continues to operate on the site, the Court stated that the NJDEP's decision to require review of an entire site, when real property comprising more than 20% of the total value of the industrial property is conveyed, is in accord with the purpose of ECRA and is a reasonable exercise of the NJDEP's discretion in implementing broad statutory language.

The Court also acknowledged that the problem of partial conveyances had been addressed by the NJDEP in order to further the legislative purpose of preventing the abandonment of industrial sites.

XIII. Constitutional Challenge to ECRA

The appellants argued that the applicability provisions of the ECRA regulations, particularly those concerning parent-subsidiary issues, violated the Commerce Clause of the United States Constitution (the "clause"). Appellants contended that the applicability provisions of the ECRA regulations directly and significantly burden interstate and international commerce. The appellants offered, by way of example of alleged impermissible burdens placed on interstate commerce, various corporate transactions in which a corporation in another state (or country) has a subsidiary or operation in New Jersey which functions as an "industrial establishment." More specifically, they reasoned that the NJDEP's ability to void a transaction for failure to comply with ECRA, unconstitutionally burdens commerce. The Court held that although the NJDEP has the power to void such out-of-state/country transactions for failure to comply with the ECRA statute, the regulation does not unconstitutionally burden interstate (or international) commerce. The Court explained that while a state law that is motivated by economic protectionism and which directly and intentionally burdens interstate commerce will almost certainly be held invalid, much more latitude is afforded state law which advances legitimate state interests. The Court concluded that ECRA furthers a legitimate local interest. It found that environmental and public health concerns, when not expressly preempted by federal law, are legitimate and compelling state concerns. The Court rejected the notion that ECRA impedes the flow of out-of-state commerce into the state and that it directly or sweepingly burdens interstate transactions. Finally, the Court found that there is no conflict with, or preemption by, federal statutes or environmental regulations.

Reprinted through courtesy of Edward A. Hogan, Esquire,
Porzio, Bromberg & Newman, Morristown, NJ, 07960.

Appendix 2

In the Clutches of the Superfund Mess

Everyone is suing everyone else—and some want to scrap the whole program.

Seven years elapsed from the time the Environmental Protection Agency identified the Helen Kramer Landfill in Mantua, N.J., as one of the nation's worst hazardous waste dumping grounds in 1982 until a $55.7 million clean-up contract was awarded. Now that work is under way, the litigation over who will pay is rapidly escalating. The Federal Government is suing 25 companies and New Jersey is suing the same companies and 25 others. A handful of these defendants have sued 239 other parties they say are responsible for most of the waste, including Philadelphia and other municipalities. And most everyone is also suing their insurance companies.

Long delays, regiments of lawyers, blizzards of documents, a widespread sense of being unfairly singled out to shoulder others' responsibilities—this is life in the clutches of the Comprehensive Environmental Response, Compensation and Liability Act of 1980, better known as Superfund. And that's when things are going smoothly, as they have by most accounts at Helen Kramer.

"Everyone misjudged how large the job was when we started," said Don R. Clay, the assistant administrator who oversees Superfund for the E.P.A.

Just as important, many groups—notably banks and municipalities—have been stunned by Superfund's reach. The law contains such broad definitions of who can be held liable for clean-up costs that they have found themselves named alongside chemical giants as defendants. Only a few banks have been named so far, but some courts have suggested that simply foreclosing on contaminated property could trigger liability. Municipalities, and hundreds of small businesses that rely on them for waste disposal, have discovered that the small amount of hazardous material in their solid waste is enough to drag them into Superfund cases.

Now, lobbyists for these groups are scurrying around Washington seeking "clarifications" of the law that would make clear that Congress never intended for them to be caught in Superfund's grip. And, to the consternation of environmental groups, some business groups are trying to harness the discontent into a frontal attack on Superfund's most basic principle, namely that those who created the nation's hazardous waste dumps should cover the cost of cleaning them up.

No-Fault System

Led by insurers and major generators of hazardous waste, these critics claim that the effort to assign responsibility at each site is adding billions of dollars to the clean-up bill and years to the timetable for getting the job done. Although they are short on specifics, they argue that some form of Government-operated no-fault system, financed by industry, is needed instead. Agreeing on the details of a no-fault proposal may well be an insurmountable challenge. Backers of the concept figure that they probably have until 1993 or even 1994 to develop a consensus. Congress ducked a debate on Superfund's effectiveness last fall with an abrupt, last-minute authorization to extend the current law through 1995.

But advocates of a no-fault system and their potential supporters may have their hand forced by banks and other lenders that are waging an active battle to gain immediate relief. Municipalities are lining up a similar drive. If either group shows signs of succeeding, a full-scale drive to dismantle Superfund's liability provisions could erupt this year.

"We aren't banging the drum to reconsider Superfund this year, but if Congress must, we want it to look at the whole thing," said Theresa Pugh, director of environmental quality at the National Association of Manufacturers, a trade group that has strongly criticized Superfund without publicly supporting the drive to replace it with a no-fault system.

There is no denying that progress to date is disappointing. The E.P.A. has more than 1,200 disposal sites on its growing National Priority List and state environmental agencies list hundreds more. While emergency clean-ups have been undertaken at more than 400 sites, only 60 or so have been cleaned up so far even though $11.2 billion overall has been spent or committed under the Superfund program. Meanwhile, "transaction costs" to pay for lawyers, multiple engineering studies and record-keeping have more than doubled the projected cost of some clean-ups.

'No Concrete Evidence'

What is far from clear, though, is whether any other approach would be substantially quicker, cheaper or fairer. "We think the law is working well," said Bill Roberts, chief lobbyist for the Environmental Defense Fund. "There's no concrete evidence that there has been a situation where people responsible for a small part of the problem pay for most of it."

Under the Superfund law, the E.P.A. is authorized to accumulate a fund to initiate clean-ups. The money comes from special taxes on industry as well as Congressional appropriations. But Congress also wanted the Government to be reimbursed for everything it spent, both to replenish the fund—which last year totaled $55 billion—and to make companies far more careful about contributing to hazardous waste problems.

So Congress armed the E.P.A. with a variety of legal weapons to get that money. The agency's atom bomb is joint and several liability, a doctrine that allows it to pin all its costs on one or more deep-pocket companies against whom it has strong evidence. Then it is up to those defendants to find and sue other parties that ought to share the burden. That includes anyone connected with owning, operating or sending waste to the site.

Insurance companies have led the way in lofting trial balloons about replacing the "polluter pays" principle with a large no-fault "environmental trust fund." Several proposals are floating around Washington about how a fund would be financed, most based on various business taxes.

"The more you tell people about how the law works today, the more shocked they are," said Linda Fuselier, a lobbyist working with the American International Group Inc., the New York-based insurance company that has been the most visible proponent of the trust fund concept.

Superfund critics are quick to concede that there is no simple answer to the nation's hazardous waste heritage. E.P.A. figures the average clean-up costs almost $30 million and some experts say the nation will eventually have to spend as much as $750 billion.

Unfair Treatment?

While agreeing that the task given the E.P.A. is overwhelming, business groups have complained from the beginning of Superfund's existence that the law leads to unfair treatment of thousands of businesses.

All too frequently, fruitless efforts to negotiate a sharing of burdens lead to litigation among hundreds of parties that drags on for years. Even mom-and-pop businesses that are eventually excused from significant payments and potential future liability because there is no record of extensive involvement in the site typically end up paying contributions of up to several thousand dollars as well as hefty attorney fees.

Not far from the Helen Kramer site, more than 400 parties are battling over responsibility for a 63-acre mountain of garbage left by Gloucester Environmental Management Services at a similar landfill. Lawyers representing different groups of defendants in negotiations spent more than $20,000 a quarter on Federal Express deliveries for three quarters simply to stay in touch with one another. "And that's with a volume discount and only using it when E.P.A. was pressing us for one or two-day turnarounds on things too thick to fax," said Jack Lynch, a New Jersey environmental lawyer who represents a number of defendants.

As the Superfund program and its litigation expenses gather momentum, the chorus of those who feel they have been sideswiped by a well-intentioned but poorly designed policy is swelling. "It's hard to measure the grumpiness index, but it has gone up," said Mr. Clay, the Superfund administrator. Mr. Clay, who is widely praised for efforts to make Superfund perform more smoothly, said that he did not feel wedded to its approach. "I think it's time to start the debate on the liability issue," he said. "But how do we make sure that we don't stop working while we have it?" He frets that companies might stop cooperating if they thought the polluter-pays standard would be dropped. "Nobody wants to be the last one shot in a war," he said.

Bankers have the best-organized campaign for narrowing the scope of the current law, but municipalities are rapidly adding pressures of their own. Lobbyists for the group agree that a municipality should be treated like any other polluter if it operated a hazardous waste site or sent substantial amounts of hazardous waste to one. But municipal officials are frightened and furious at court rulings that have interpreted Superfund broadly enough to include towns and cities in cases where they sent common garbage to private landfills or simply licensed private carters.

The E.P.A. agreed not to pursue municipalities in such cases in 1989, but that has not stopped private parties sued by the E.P.A. from doing so. In one notorious case, a Federal judge ruled last December that 64 companies sued by the E.P.A. have a right to sue 29 Los Angeles suburbs for 90 percent of a clean-up that could cost more than $800 million. At the Los Angeles landfill and similar sites, which make up about 20 percent of the Superfund priority list, the companies involved concede that the waste from the municipalities contains just a small percentage of hazardous substances, less than 1 percent of the volume of the municipalities' garbage, by most estimates. But the companies argue that the garbage accounts for most of the waste at those sites and dictates the nature of the clean-up that will be required.

General Plant Trash

Such arguments make environmentalists, representatives of the municipalities and some enforcement officials seethe.

"We don't pursue industry for sending general plant trash to a site," said John MacDonald, assistant section chief in the hazardous site litigation section of the New Jersey Attorney General's office. "And industry always tells us they sent no hazardous wastes to the site when we inquire in such cases, even though general plant trash contains the same kinds of things that they say justifies bringing municipalities in."

The long-term goal of the corporate defendants, say the environmentalists and other groups, is to spread the pain of Superfund so widely that pressure builds to abandon the polluter-pays standard altogether. In the shorter term, the presence of financially strapped but politically potent parties like cities adds to the pressure on E.P.A. to select less expensive clean-up plans.

"The corporations not only want the cities' pockets but also to have them as front men in arguing with the E.P.A. on clean-up standards," said David Kolker, an attorney with Speigel & McDiarmid, a Washington law firm that represents American Communities for Clean-up Equity, a coalition campaigning to limit liability.

The lenders and municipalities must contend with opposition from two directions: from business groups that oppose any relief that might reduce the pressure for sweeping change and from environmental groups that believe Superfund's liability provisions are basically sound in their current form.

Mr. Roberts at the Environmental Defense Fund, for example, said that his group and other environmentalists support clarification of the rules governing lender liability in cases where banks exerted no control over polluters' operations. But, he said, the legislative relief sought by the banks goes much further than that.

Such Superfund defenders say that the polluter-pays principle, however unfair it may be in some cases, sends an important precautionary message to American industry. They also argue that proposed no-fault funds would unwisely cap what the nation had available to spend on clean-ups. And they say that the involvement of private parties provides a necessary check on the E.P.A.

More Data Needed

Everyone on both sides of the argument agrees on the need for more data. One eagerly awaited study is an investigation by the Rand Corporation's Institute of Civil Justice, due out this summer, on transaction costs. And Resources for the Future, a Washington-based think tank, is working on a list of criteria, such as fairness and speed of clean-up, that it hopes can serve as a basis for measuring the strengths and weaknesses of Superfund and alternative approaches. Resources for the Future also wants to do a profile of the National Priority List, characterizing sites by how many parties are involved, among other things.

"We need to know when we hear an anecdote whether it applies to 20 percent of the sites or 80 percent of them," said Katherine Probst, a Resources policy analyst. "If we could all agree on what we are talking about, it would be helpful."

Controlling the Litigation

The biggest Superfund sites are not necessarily the ones that raise the starkest questions about the act's fairness.

Such sites often involve a group of experienced defendants who work with the Environmental Protection Agency and one another to keep clean-ups on track.

"The transaction costs at Helen Kramer have been minimized so far," said William H. Hyatt, Jr., a veteran Superfund attorney, ticking off several procedures that have been used to keep legal fees down at the Helen Kramer Landfill in Mantua, N.J., one of the largest dump sites.

Mr. Hyatt noted that the original defendants could have added at least 100 more parties to the case than they actually did, perhaps as many as 300 more. Mr. Hyatt is the liaison between the judge handling the litigation and the chemical companies and other large concerns that were in the original group of defendants.

"We deliberately excluded those we felt had minimal involvement," Mr. Hyatt said.

By contrast, two Superfund defendants at the small Ludlow site near Utica, N.Y., have dragged 600 parties into their dispute, including local restaurants, nursing homes and school districts.

Often, the links that pull small companies into Superfund's clutches are extremely tenuous. Chudnow Iron and Metal, a Milwaukee scrap recycler, says that it has been linked to a contaminated landfill in Racine, Wis., on the strength of an entry in the landfill owner's address book. "I think it's there because we bought scrap from him," said Larry Chudnow, president of the family-owned company.

"In the Clutches of the Superfund Mess," by Barnaby J. Feder, has been reprinted with permission of *The New York Times,* New York City, NY. It originally appeared June 16, 1991,

Appendix 3

ECRA-001
4/90

NEW JERSEY DEPARTMENT OF ENVIRONMENTAL PROTECTION
DIVISION OF HAZARDOUS WASTE MANAGEMENT
INDUSTRIAL SITE EVALUATION ELEMENT
CN 028, TRENTON, N.J. 08625-0028

ENVIRONMENTAL CLEANUP RESPONSIBILITY ACT (ECRA)

INITIAL NOTICE

GENERAL INFORMATION SUBMISSION (GIS)

This is the first part of a two-part application form. This information must be submitted within 5 days following any applicable situation as specified at N.J. A. C. 7:26B-1.5 or any triggering event as specified at N.J. A. C. 7:26B-1.6. Please refer to the instructions and N.J.A.C. 7:26B-3.2 before filling out this form. Answer all questions. Should you encounter any problems in completing this form, we recommend that you discuss the matter with a representative from the Element. Submitting insufficient data may cause processing delays and possible postponement of your transaction. Please call (609) 633-7141 between the hours of 8:30 a.m. and 4:30 p.m. to request assistance.

PLEASE TYPE OR PRINT

Date_____

1. A. Industrial Establishment

    Name_____ Telephone #_(_____)_____

    Street Address _____

    City of Town _____ State _____ Zip Code _____

    Municipality _____ County _____

  B. Tax Block Number(s)_____ Tax Lot Number(s) _____

    _____   _____

  C. Standard Industrial Classification (SIC) Number _____

  D. Current Property Owner(s)

    Name _____ Telephone # __(_____)_____

    Firm _____

    Street Address _____

    Municipality _____ State _____ Zip Code _____

  E. Current Business Operator(s) of Industrial Establishment

    Name _____ Telephone # __(_____)_____

    Firm _____

    Street Address _____

    Municipality _____ State _____ Zip Code _____

238 *Victim*

ECRA-001
4/90

F. Current Business Owner(s)

Name _____ Telephone # _(____)_____

Firm _____

Street Address _____

Municipality _____ State _____ Zip Code _____

G. Have there been any previous ECRA submissions (including Applicability Determinations) by this Industrial Establishment or another Industrial Establishment which occupied the same tax block and lot number?

_____ Yes _____ No

If Yes, Name of Industrial Establishment _____

ECRA Case No. _____ Date Submitted _____

Current Status _____

2. Describe the transaction in terms of the action which initiates the ECRA review. (See N.J.A.C. 7:26B-1.5&1.6)

_____

_____

_____

3. Is a cessation of operations involved at this location? _____ Yes _____ No

If Yes, give the date of public release of the decision to close the facility. Date ____/____/____

Is a copy of the public release enclosed? _____ Yes _____ No

If No, state the reason _____

_____

_____

4. If the transaction initiating an ECRA review is an agreement of sale or execution of an option to purchase, fill in the date of execution of that instrument plus provide one (1) copy of the document. Date_____

A. Is a sale involved? _____ Yes _____ No (If no, skip 4B, C and D.)

B. Date of Agreement/Letter of Intent/Notifications of Option to Purchase ____/____/____

C. Is a copy of the agreement of sale or option to purchase enclosed? _____ Yes _____ No

If No, state the reason _____

ECRA-001
4/90

D. List other parties (purchasers) to the transaction:

NAME	STREET ADDRESS & MUNICIPALITY	PHONE NO.
_____	_____	_____
	_____	
	_____	
_____	_____	_____
	_____	
	_____	
_____	_____	_____
	_____	
	_____	

5. Date proposed for closure of operations or transfer of title _____

6. Authorized agent designated to work with the Department

Name _____ Telephone # _(_____)_____

Firm _____

Street Address _____

Municipality _____ State _____ Zip Code _____

240 *Victim*

ECRA-001
4/90

CERTIFICATIONS:

A. The following certification shall be signed by the highest ranking individual at the site with overall responsibility for that site or activity. Where there is no individual at the site with overall responsibility for that site or activity, this certification shall be signed by the individual having responsibility for the overall operation of the site or activity.

I certify under penalty of law that the information provided in this document is true, accurate and complete. I am aware that there are significant civil penalties for knowingly submitting false, inaccurate or incomplete information and that I am committing a crime of the fourth degree if I make a written false statement which I do not believe to be true. I am also aware that if I knowingly direct or authorize the violation of N.J.S.A. 13:1K-6 et seq., I am personally liable for the penalties set forth at N.J.S.A. 13:1K-13.

Typed/Printed Name _____ Title _____

Signature _____ Date _____

Sworn to and Subscribed Before Me
on this _____
Date of _____ 19 ____

_____
Notary

B. The following certification shall be signed as follows:

1. For a corporation, by a principal executive officer of at least the level of vice president;
2. For a partnership or sole proprietorship, by a general partner or the proprietor, respectively; or
3. For a municipality, State, Federal or other public agency, by either a principal executive officer or ranking elected official.

I certify under penalty of law that I have personally examined and am familiar with the information submitted in this application and all attached documents, and that based on my inquiry of those individuals immediately responsible for obtaining the information, I believe that the submitted information is true, accurate and complete. I am aware that there are significant civil penalties for knowingly submitting false, inaccurate, or incomplete information and that I am committing a crime of the fourth degree if I make a written false statement which I do not believe to be true. I am also aware that if I knowingly direct or authorize the violation of N.J.S.A. 13:1K-6 et seq., I am personally liable for the penalties set forth at N.J.S.A. 13:1K-13.

Typed/Printed Name _____ Title _____

Signature _____ Date _____

Sworn to and Subscribed Before Me
on this _____
Date of _____ 19 ____

_____
Notary

ECRA-002
12/87

NEW JERSEY DEPARTMENT OF ENVIRONMENTAL PROTECTION
DIVISION OF HAZARDOUS WASTE MANAGEMENT
INDUSTRIAL SITE EVALUATION ELEMENT
CN 028, TRENTON, N.J. 08625

ENVIRONMENTAL CLEANUP RESPONSIBILITY ACT (ECRA)

INITIAL NOTICE

SITE EVALUATION SUBMISSION (SES)

This is the second part of a two-part application form. This information must be submitted within 45 days following any applicable situation as specified at N.J.A.C. 7:26B-1.5 or any triggering event as specified at N.J.A.C. 7:26B-1.6. Please refer to the instructions and N.J.A.C. 7:26B-3.2 before filling out this form. Answer all questions. Should you encounter any problems in completing this form, we recommend that you discuss the matter with a representative from the Element. Submitting incorrect or insufficient data may cause processing delays and possible postponement of your transaction. Please call (609) 633-7141 between the hours of 8:30 a.m. and 4:30 p.m. to request assistance.

PLEASE PRINT OR TYPE

Date_____

1. Industrial Establishment

   Name _____

   Address _____

   City or Town _____ Zip Code _____

   Municipality _____ County _____

A. Operational and Ownership History: *(Attach additional sheets if necessary)*

Name	Owner/ Operator	From	To	Current Address
_____	_____	_____	_____	_____
_____	_____	_____	_____	_____
_____	_____	_____	_____	_____
_____	_____	_____	_____	_____

B. Brief description of past operation(s) conducted on site *(Attach additional sheets if necessary)*

_____

_____

_____

_____

Page 1 of 8

ECRA-002
12/87

2. List all federal and state environmental permits applied for, or received, or both, at this facility *(Attach additional sheets if necessary)*

Check here if no permits are involved _____

A. New Jersey Bureau of Air Pollution Control

Permit Number	Certificate Number	Date of Approval or Denial	Reason for Denial (if applicable)	Expiration Date
_____	_____	_____	_____	_____
			_____	
_____	_____	_____	_____	_____
			_____	
_____	_____	_____	_____	_____
			_____	

B. New Jersey Pollutant Discharge Elimination System (NJPDES)

Number	Discharge Activity	Date Issued or Denied	Expiration Date	Body of Water Discharged Into
_____	_____	_____	_____	_____
_____	_____	_____	_____	_____

C. United State Environmental Protection Agency (EPA) Identification Number and copy of the most recent generator Annual Report prepared pursuant to the New Jersey Hazardous Waste Regulations. *(If applicable)*

ID # _____

Is a copy of the Annual Report attached? _____ Yes (See Attachment #_____) _____ No

D. Resource, Conservation, Recovery Act (RCRA) Permit # _____

E. Bureau of Underground Storage Tank Registration Number(s) _____

F. All other federal, state, local governmental permits.

Agency Issuing Permit	Permit No.	Date of Approval or Denial	Expiration Date
_____	_____	_____	_____
_____	_____	_____	_____
_____	_____	_____	_____
_____	_____	_____	_____

ECRA-002
12/87

3. Summary of Enforcement Actions for Violation of Environmental Laws or Regulations:

Check here if no enforcement actions are involved _____

A. Date of Action _____

Section of Law or Statute violated _____

Type of Enforcement Action _____

Description of the Violation _____

_____

_____

_____

_____

How was the violation resolved? _____

_____

_____

_____

_____

_____

B. Date of Action _____

Section of Law or Statute violated _____

Type of Enforcement Action _____

Description of the Violation _____

_____

_____

_____

_____

How was the violation resolved? _____

_____

_____

_____

_____

_____

4. Site Map

Is this map enclosed? _____ Yes (See Attachment #_____) _____ No

If No, state the reason _____

_____

_____

(Attach additional pages, if necessary)

244 *Victim*

ECRA-002
12/87

5. Decription of Operations:

   Is this report enclosed?   _____ Yes (See Attachment #_____)   _____ No

   If No, state the reason _____

   _____

   _____

6. Description of Building Heating System:

   A. How is the Industrial Establishment currently heated? (Oil, Gas, Electric) _____

   How long has the Industrial Establishment been heated by the above fuel/energy source: _____years

   B. Was the Industrial Establishment heated by fuel oil at any time: _____Yes   _____No

   Is information on the decommissioning of underground fuel oil tanks included with item No. 14 of this form?

   _____Yes   _____No   If no, explain below: _____

   _____

   _____

   C. Are the results of the Integrity Evaluation for Existing Underground Fuel Oil Tanks enclosed?

   _____Yes (See Attachment #_____)   _____No   If no, state the reason _____

   _____

   _____

7. Summary of Industrial Establishment Wastewater Discharges of Sanitary and/or Industrial Waste:

   A. **Discharge Period**

From	To	Discharge Type	Treatment By
_____	Present	_____	_____
_____	_____	_____	_____
_____	_____	_____	_____

   B. If the Industrial Establishment discharges sanitary and/or industrial wastes to a publicly-owned treatment plant, provide the name/address of that facility.

   Name_____   Telephone # _____

   Street Address _____

   Municipality _____   State _____   Zip Code _____

Date(s) of Discharge	Nature of Discharge
1. _____	_____
2. _____	_____
3. _____	_____

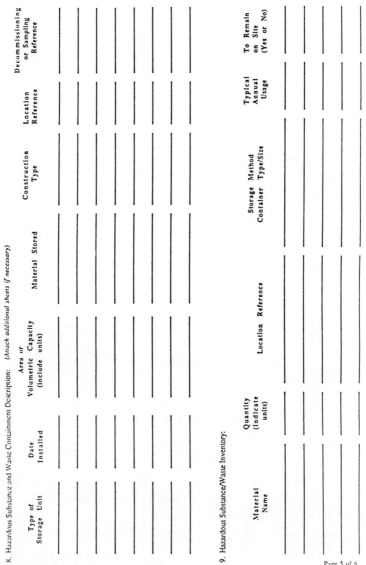

8. Hazardous Substance and Waste Containment Description: *(Attach additional sheets if necessary)*

Type of Storage Unit	Date Installed	Area or Volumetric Capacity (Include units)	Material Stored	Construction Type	Location Reference	Decommissioning or Sampling Reference

9. Hazardous Substance/Waste Inventory:

Material Name	Quantity (Indicate units)	Location Reference	Storage Method Container Type/Size	Typical Annual Usage	To Remain on Site (Yes or No)

246 *Victim*

ECRA-002
12/87

10. Discharge History of Hazardous Substances and Wastes:

   A. Have there been <u>any</u> discharges of hazardous substances and wastes?
      _____Yes (Complete Item B below)   _____No (Go to Item 10C)

   B. Summary of Discharges and Resolutions

<u>Description of Discharge Event</u>	<u>Response and Resolutions</u>

   C. Is this Industrial Establishment subject to Spill Prevention Control and Countermeasure (SPCC) per 40 CFR Part 112 or Discharge Prevention, Containment and Countermeasure (DPCC) Plan per NJAC 7:1E-4.1 requirements?

      _____Yes _____No   A copy of the Plan(s) may be required at the discretion of the Department.

11. Sampling Plan Proposal

   A. Is sampling proposed at the facility?   _____Yes (See Attachment #_____)   No_____

      If sampling is not proposed, please explain below. *(Attach additional sheets if necessary)*

   B. Is groundwater sampling proposed?   _____Yes   _____No

      <u>Note:</u> If groundwater sampling is proposed under the plan, you must complete ECRA Form 002A "Request for Hydrogeologic Assessment" and submit it with the application.

ECRA-002
12/87

12. Decontamination/Decommissioning Plan

    A. Is the facility Decontamination/Decommissioning Plan enclosed?

        _____Yes (See Attachment #_____) _____No

    B. If no, specify why decontamination/decommissioning is not considered necessary.

_____

_____ _____

_____

_____

13. Historical Data on environmental quality at the Industrial Establishment

    A. Were sampling results obtained on Environmental Quality for the Industrial Establishment?

        _____Yes (See Attachment #_____) _____No

    B. If sampling results were obtained but are not part of this application, please explain below:

_____

_____

_____

_____

14. List any other information you are submitting or which has been formally requested by the Department:

Description	**Attachment #**
_____	_____
_____	_____
_____	_____
_____	_____

FEE CHECKLIST

Include below a breakdown of the total fee submitted with this application. (See N.J.A.C. 7:26B-1.10 for the appropriate fees.)

Item	**Amount ($)**
1. Initial Notice Review	
i. Without Sampling Plan	
ii. With Sampling Plan that includes only underground	
storage tank analysis without groundwater monitoring	_____
iii. With Sampling Plan other than ii. above or iv. below	_____
iv. With Sampling Plan that includes any groundwater monitoring	_____
2. Sampling Data Review	_____
3. Negative Declaration Review	_____
4. Cleanup Plan Review	_____
5. Oversight of Cleanup Plan Implementation	_____
TOTAL FEE ENCLOSED	$_____

ARE FEES ENCLOSED? _____YES

248 *Victim*

ECRA-002
12/87

CERTIFICATIONS:

A. The following certification shall be signed by the highest ranking individual at the site with overall responsibility for that site or activity. Where there is no individual at the site with overall responsibility for that site or activity, this certification shall be signed by the individual having responsibility for the overall operation of the site or activity.

I certify under penalty of law that the information provided in this document is true, accurate and complete: I am aware that there are significant civil penalties for knowingly submitting false, inaccurate or incomplete information and that I am committing a crime of the fourth degree if I make a written false statement which I do not believe to be true. I am also aware that if I knowingly direct or authorize the violation of N.J.S.A. 13:1K-6 et seq., I am personally liable for the penalties set forth at N.J.S.A. 13:1K-8.

Typed/Printed Name _____   Title _____

Signature _____   Date _____

Sworn to and Subscribed Before Me
on this _____
Date of _____ 19 ____

_____
Notary

B. The following certification shall be signed as follows:

1. For a corporation, by a principal executive officer of at least the level of vice president;
2. For a partnership or sole proprietorship, by a general partner or the proprietor, respectively; or
3. For a municipality, State, Federal or other public agency, by either a principal executive officer or ranking elected official.

I certify under penalty of law that I have personally examined and am familiar with the information submitted in this application and all attached documents, and that based on my inquiry of those individuals immediately responsible for obtaining the information, I believe that the submitted information is true, accurate and complete. I am aware that there are significant civil penalties for knowingly submitting false, inaccurate, or incomplete information and that I am committing a crime of the fourth degree if I make a written false statement which I do not believe to be true. I am also aware that if I knowingly direct or authorize the violation of N.J.S.A. 13:1K-6 et seq., I am personally liable for the penalties set forth at N.J.S.A. 13:1K-8.

Typed/Printed Name _____   Title _____

Signature _____   Date _____

Sworn to and Subscribed Before Me
on this _____
Date of _____ 19 ____

_____
Notary

ECRA-009
9/90

NEW JERSEY DEPARTMENT OF ENVIRONMENTAL PROTECTION
DIVISION OF HAZARDOUS WASTE MANAGEMENT
INDUSTRIAL SITE EVALUATION ELEMENT
CN 028, TRENTON, N.J. 08625-0028

ENVIRONMENTAL CLEANUP RESPONSIBILITY ACT (ECRA)

APPLICABILITY/NONAPPLICABILITY AFFIDAVIT

The purpose of this Affidavit is to obtain an Applicability/Nonapplicability Determination from the New Jersey Department of Environmental Protection pursuant to the Environmental Cleanup Responsibility Act, N.J. S.A. 13:1K-6 et seq. and N.J.A.C. 7:26B-1.9. Fee is $200.00.

NOTE: *All sections of this application shall be completed or it will be returned.*

PLEASE TYPE OR PRINT

Date _____

A. Determination of Applicability/Nonapplicability should be mailed to the following:

Name _____
Address _____
City of Town _____ County _____
State _____ Zip Code _____ Tele. No. _____

B. Name of Business _____
Standard Industrial Classification (SIC) Number _____

C. Property Location for which request is being transmitted:

Street Address _____
Tax Block(s) _____ Tax Lot(s) _____
Municipality _____ County _____
State _____ Zip Code _____

D. Transaction for which the Applicability/Nonapplicability Determination is requested: *(Check appropriate transaction)*
* Please attach a detailed description of these transactions.
** Please attach the most recent Consolidated Financial Statements for all companies involved in the proposed transaction.

1. _____ Sale of Property
2. _____ Sale of Business
3. _____ Business Ceasing Operations
4. _____ Refinancing/Construction Loan
5. _____ Sale of Stock in Corporation*
6. _____ Condemnation
   _____ Other: *(Explain)* _____

7. _____ Bankruptcy
8. _____ Corporate Merger*
9. _____ Partnership Situation Change*
10. _____ Intra Family
11. _____ Corporate Reorganization**
12. _____ Sale of Assets**

Date of Planned Transaction: _____

Purchaser:

Name _____
Address _____
City or Town _____ County _____
State _____ Zip Code _____

1

250   *Victim*

ECRA-009
9/90

E. Operations:

1.) The property owner and/or operator must completely describe in detail the operations and processes conducted at the site including a list of all tenants, their operations and processes, occupying any part of the property since December 31, 1983. *(Attach additional sheets, if necessary.)*

_____

_____

_____

_____

2.) If the property described above is vacant land, is this property contiguous to other property under the control of the person or business described in F below: ___ Yes   ___ No

F. Current Owner of the Property for which an Applicability/Nonapplicability Determination is requested:

Name_____

Street Address _____ Municipality _____

State _____ Zip Code _____ Tele. No.   (_____)_____

G. History:

1. Previous Owners and history of on-site operations since December 31, 1983 *(Attach additional sheets, if necessary):*

Name   **Address**   **Date/Operations**

2. Is this site currently or has this site previously been the subject of any other ECRA review? *Please submit copies of previous submittals or approvals.*

____Previous LNA Application   ____Negative Declaration
____Administrative Consent Order   ____Approved Cleanup Plan
____Active Case   ____No prior ECRA Review

H. Hazardous Substances or Wastes: (This information is only required if the facility or business has a subject SIC.)

List all types and quantities of hazardous substances or wastes including petroleum products that are generated, manufactured, refined, transported, treated, stored, handled or disposed at the property, both above and below ground, which are included in the Department's "Unified Hazardous Substance List" and any amount of any waste substances required to be reported to the Department on special waste manifest forms pursuant to N.J.A.C. 7:26-7.4, designated as a hazardous waste pursuant to N.J.A.C. 7:26-7.4, designated as a hazardous waste pursuant to N.J.A.C. 7:26-8, or as otherwise provided by law. *(Attach additional sheets if necessary.)*

_____

_____

_____

I. How is the building(s) heated? *(Oil, Gas, Electric)*   If Oil, how many tanks? _____
   Storage Capacity of each _____   Above or below ground _____

J. Was the building(s) ever heated by oil? ___ Yes   ___ No   If so, when? _____

2

ECRA-009
9/90

K. CERTIFICATIONS:

1. The following certification shall be signed by the highest ranking individual at the site with overall responsibility for that site or activity. Where there is no individual at the site with overall responsibility for that site or activity, this certification shall be signed by the individual having responsibility for the overall operation of the site or activity.

I certify under penalty of law that the information provided in this document is true, accurate and complete. I am aware that there are significant civil penalties for knowingly submitting false, inaccurate or incomplete information and that I am committing a crime of the fourth degree if I make a written false statement which I do not believe to be true. I am also aware that if I knowingly direct or authorize the violation of N.J.S.A. 13:1K-6 et seq., I am personally liable for the penalties set forth at N.J.S.A. 13:1K-13.

Typed/Printed Name _____   Title _____

Signature _____   Date _____

Company _____

Sworn to and Subscribed Before Me
on this _____
Date of _____ 19 ____

_____
Notary

2. The following certification shall be signed as follows:
    1. For a corporation, by a principal executive officer of at least the level of vice president;
    2. For a partnership or sole proprietorship, by a general partner or the proprietor, respectively; or
    3. For a municipality, State, Federal or other public agency, by either a principal executive officer or ranking elected official.

I certify under penalty of law that I have personally examined and am familiar with the information submitted in this application and all attached documents, and that based on my inquiry of those individuals immediately responsible for obtaining the information, I believe that the submitted information is true, accurate and complete. I am aware that there are significant civil penalties for knowingly submitting false, inaccurate, or incomplete information and that I am committing a crime of the fourth degree if I make a written false statement which I do not believe to be true. I am also aware that if I knowingly direct or authorize the violation of N.J.S.A. 13:1K-6 et seq., I am personally liable for the penalties set forth at N.J.S.A. 13:1K-13.

Typed/Printed Name _____   Title _____

Signature _____   Date _____

Company _____

Sworn to and Subscribed Before Me
on this _____
Date of _____ 19 ____

_____
Notary

Have you enclosed a check or money order for $200? _____ Yes _____ No

3

Appendix 4

WARREN COUNTY ECONOMIC DEVELOPMENT ADVISORY COUNCIL RECOMMENDED TO BOARD OF CHOSEN FREEHOLDERS REGARDING ENVIRONMENTAL CLEAN-UP RESPONSIBILITY ACT AND RELATED ENVIRONMENTAL RESTRICTIVE LAWS, RULES AND REGULATIONS

Because New Jersey's Department of Environmental Protection, and the State's ECRA Act have gained a reputation throughout the United States, and even abroad, as deterrents and obstacles to the continued consideration of the state as a site for new or expanding industry, and,

Because delays in DEP administration of regulations and applications of ECRA provisions have put undue economic hardship on many property owners and companies and caused usable properties to be vacant for long periods of time, and,

Because financial institutions and lending authorities use ECRA and other environmental considerations as a reason for delaying or declining requests for capital,

The Economic Development Advisory Council recommends that the Warren County Board of Chosen Freeholders urges legislators of the 23rd and 24th Legislative District, other key legislators and responsible personnel within Governor Florio's administration to expedite any economic impact study on the cost to New Jersey industry in fees, engineering and consulting costs, and the cost to the state in lost business and new plants, as opposed to the actual clean-up that has transpired, and, that amended legislation be proposed, if required, to balance the costs in economic development to the benefits accrued; and that reorganization of the DEP go forward as fast as possible with the objective of reducing the time and morass of red tape required to obtain permits.

SUBSTANTIATING REMARKS

Two companies which relocated from Warren County to Pennsylvania told State and County economic development representatives that one of their primary reasons for leaving the state was the DEP and the direction of state government;

Nine companies in Warren County told State and County economic development representatives they would not consider expanding in New Jersey primarily because of DEP provisions, and the direction of state government;

One major company which decided in 1987 to expand in Warren County told State and County economic development representatives they regretted the decision to expand here, and that their home office in Germany has instructed them to look elsewhere for future expansion. Their application to the state for on-site septic system was made in 1987. (The public notice was just published on July 4, 1991. There is a 30-day period for objections. Next step is for treatment works approval before building can begin. Construction will take approximately one month, then an application must be made for operational approval.) (The company hopes to have the system operational before winter sets in.);

Fifty thousand dollars in application fees and consulting/engineering fees and 2-1/2 years before a small printing business could change hands. (No clean-up was required for the site, and all trace chemicals were within limits);

Eighteen months to obtain a stream crossing permit by a local utility, and three hours to complete the work;

A major company employing nearly 1000 people in Warren County noted that New Jersey was not considered for a $60 million expansion because of DEP considerations. (That firm's request for modification to an existing cogeneration system, which would benefit air quality, took 2-1/2 years to get DEP approval);

A request by another major company employing more than 1000 people in Warren County to bring a cogeneration system on line took two years for approval. Officials of the company have told county economic development representatives that new products added to the company's line will not be produced in New Jersey. That company was also cited with a fine for parking lot run-off with newspaper headlines noting $1 million fine.

Another major company employing nearly 1000 people in Warren County is on record in a newspaper quote that it will not expand in New Jersey because of ECRA. That company is also tearing down nearly a million square feet of office and industrial space and landfilling on site. The company also has 150 acres of virgin lands, among the best industrial acreage in Warren County, that it will not offer for development because of ECRA.

Clorox, which had sought sites in New Jersey for a period of three years, including four tracts in Warren County, rejected all state sites on the basis of DEP consideration and selected Maryland for their new plant. As a result, their Jersey City plant will be closed and 180 people will be unemployed.

A 20,000 square foot industrial building went on the market and closed in 1986 for $375,000 after the seller obtained a $500,000 bond. So far the owner has spent nearly $400,000 in fees and lawyers/consultants costs and has not yet obtained an approved clean-up plan. In one case, it took the DEP 16 months to respond to information submitted.

Warren County Economic Development Advisory Council, Recommendation dated 7/17/91, distributed at a public hearing in Phillipsburg, New Jersey.

Appendix 5

ECRA Fee Structure as of 8/21/89

	Standard	Small Business
1. Inital Notice Review		
a. Without Sampling Plan	$ 2,000.00	$ 750.00
b. With Sampling Plan that includes		
underground storage tank analysis	3,000.00	1,500.00
c. With Sampling Plan other than b		
above or d below	5,000.00	3,000.00
d. With Sampling Plan that includes		
any ground water monitoring	7,500.00	4,500.00
2. Sampling Data Review	1,000.00	1,000.00
3. Negative Declaration Review	500.00	250.00
4. Clean-up Plan Review		
(Based on cost of clean-up)		
a. $1 - $9,999	1,000.00	1,000.00
b. $10,000 - $99,999	2,500.00	2,500.00
c. $100,000 - $499,999	5,000.00	5,000.00
d. $500,000 - $999,999	8,000.00	8,000.00
e. Over $1,000,000	11,000.00	11,000.00
5. Oversight of Clean-up Plan		
Implementation (based on cost of clean-up)		
a. $1 - $9,999	1,000.00	1,000.00
b. $10,000 - $99,999	3,000.00	3,000.00
c. $100,000 - $499,999	7,000.00	7,000.00
d. $500,000 - $999,999	10,000.00	10,000.00
e. Over $1,000,000	12,000.00	12,000.00
6. Applicability Determination	200.00	200.00
7. De Minimus Quantity Exemption	300.00	300.00
8. Limited Conveyance Review	500.00	250.00
9. Administrative Consent Order	2,000.00	2,000.00
10. ACO Amendment	500.00	500.00
11. Confidentiality Claim	350.00	350.00

Small business means any business which is resident in this State, independently owned and operated and not dominant in its field,, and which employs fewer than 100 full time employees.

The schedule for submission of fees shall be as follows:

1. The Initial Notice review fee based upon the applicable sampling plan category shall be submitted with the Site Evaluation Submission (SES).

2. Any sampling data submitted to the Department shall be accompanied by the appropriate fee. Data submitted for no more than 3 underground storage tank integrity tests, if that is the only sampling data submitted to the Department, shall not be assessed a sampling data review fee.

3. Any negative declaration submission shall be accompanied by the appropriate fee.

4. Any draft clean-up plan or partial clean-up plan submitted shall be accompanied by the clean-up plan review fee based upon the estimated clean-up cost contained in the draft clean-up plan.

a. If the approved clean-up plan cost estimate or actual clean-up cost is in a higher fee category, the owner or operator shall submit a payment for the difference in the fees within 30 days of issuance of clean-up plan approval or with the final report on clean-up implementation, whichever is appropriate. If the actual clean-up cost is in a lower fee category, a refund will be issued by the Department within 90 days of issuance of a letter of full compliance.

5. The clean-up plan oversight fee shall be paid within 14 days from the receipt of the Department's clean-up plan approval letter and shall be based upon the estimated clean-up cost contained in the clean-up plan.

a. If the actual clean-up cost is in a higher fee category, the owner or operator shall submit a payment for the difference in the fees with the final report on clean-up implementation. If the actual clean-up cost is in a lower fee category, a refund will be issued by the Department within 90 days of issuance of a letter of full compliance.

6. Any request for an applicability determination shall be accompanied by the appropriate fee.

7. Any request for a de Minimus quantity exemption shall be accompanied by the appropriate fee.

8. Any request for a Certificate of Limited Conveyance shall be accompanied by the appropriate fee.

9. Any request for an ACO shall be accompanied by the appropriate fee.

Extracted from official ECRA Fee Submission Schedule, NJDEPE,
Division of Hazardous Waste Management,
Trenton, New Jersey 08625

Notes

Chapter I

1. "Fairmount Plant Made Bombs During the War," *Observer-Tribune* (Chester, N.J.), July 27, 1989.
2. Joseph Douglass, Letter to Author, September 5, 1989.
3. *Observer-Tribune,* July 27, 1989.
4. Phil Crammer, "Letter to the Editor," *Observer-Tribune,* August 31, 1989.
5. Thomas Kean, "Letter to the Author," June 9, 1988.
6. *Observer-Tribune,* July 27, 1989.
7. Ibid.
8. Rick Butler, "EPA Wraps Up 9 Month Cleanup at Morris Site," *The Star Ledger,* Newark, N.J., November 19, 1991.
9. Rick Butler, "Clean-Up of Toxic Waste at Industrial Site to Begin," *The Star Ledger,* February 28, 1991.
10. Eric Schmuckler, "Dangerous Criminal Nabbed," Forbes, January 22, 1990. Reprinted by permission.
11. Cyril Francus, Secretary-Treasurer, C & M Manufacturing Co., Fort Lee, N.J., Letter, February 5, 1990.
12. Ibid.
13. Kathy B. Carter, "Cleanup Laws Put Many Landowners in a Bind," *The Star Ledger,* April 8, 1990.
14. Ibid.
15. Ibid.
16. "Grand Jury Indicts Executive," *The Star Ledger,* February 17, 1991, p. 40.

17. "Leaves Roll into Lake Bring Fine to Homeowner," *Observer-Tribune,* November 9, 1989.
18. Commerce & Industry Association, "ECRA Survey," February 1990.
19. Ibid.
20. Frank A. Langella, "Letter to the Author," February 1990.
21. Arthur Albohn, "Letter to the Author," December 7, 1988.

Chapter II

1. Amy H. Berger, "The ECRA Mess," *Success Magazine,* January 1990.
2. "Showdown Nearing on Rules for Cleanup of Industrial Sites," *The Star Ledger,* December 11, 1988.
3. Debra K. Rudin, "ENR News, Hazardous Waste," *McGraw Hill Construction Weekly,* April 13, 1989.
4. Amy H. Berger, "The ECRA Mess."
5. Ronald J. Brandmayr, Jr., "Forum," *The Star Ledger,* April 25, 1990.
6. Commerce & Industry Association, "Survey," February 1990.
7. Judith Yaskin, "Critic of the DEP is Taken to Task," *The Star Ledger,* October 21, 1990.

Chapter III

1. Barbara Grady, "Keystone Buyer Won't Re-open Plant," *The Record* (Hackensack, N.J.), June 18, 1991. Reprinted with permission.
2. Jack Lyne, "Westinghouse's Allen Wood," *Site Selection Magazine,* October 1988.
3. Commerce & Industry Association, "Survey," February 1990.
4. David O'Johnson, "A Printer's Trip through Environmental Quicksand," *Printing Manager,* March 1986. Published by the National Association of Printers and Lithographers, Teaneck, New Jersey.

5. *Daily Record* (Morris County, N.J.), "Environmental Cleanup Law Unfair to Small Business," April 19, 1988.
6. *Daily Record,* March 12, 1988.
7. Commerce & Industry Association, "Survey," February 1990.
8. Tom Johnson, "RCA Posts Bond," *The Star Ledger,* June 25, 1986.
9. Commerce & Industry Association, "Survey," February 1990.
10. Joseph R. Douglass, "A Practical Look at ECRA," *N. J. Industrial News,* July, 1988.
11. John T. Harding, "Redevelopment Cleanup," *The Star Ledger,* May 29, 1988.
12. "Showdown Nearing on Rules for Cleanup of Industrial Sites," *The Star Ledger,* December 11, 1988.
13. Richard S. Beltram, "Letters to the Editor," *Business Journal of New Jersey,* December 1990.
14. Donald D. Merino, "Study" (Hoboken, N.J.), Stevens Institute of Technology, 1989.
15. Edward C. Croot, Letter to Author, June 11, 1991.
16. Hannock Weissman, Roseland, N.J., "Law Update," April 1991.

Chapter IV

1. "Towns Shy Away From Litter Plan Tied in Red Tape," *The Star Ledger,* February 13, 1989.
2. "Red Tape Tangles Housing," *The Star Ledger,* February 12, 1989.
3. "New Gas Tank Rules Will Force Stations to Close," *Observer-Tribune,* February 16, 1989.
4. "EPA Moves to Fine 3 Jersey Firms," *The Star Ledger,* January 11, 1989.
5. "Polluting Cars Can Be Reported," *Observer-Tribune,* January 19, 1989.

6. "Perth Amboy is Fined $686,000 for Water Treatment Violations," *The Star Ledger,* January 26, 1989.
7. "Toxics Disclosure Rules Gaining in Real Estate Deals," *McGraw-Hill's ENR,* April 13, 1989.
8. "Roxbury Disputes DEP Fine," *The Star Ledger,* March 1, 1990.
9. Tom Johnson, "Help is on the Way," *The Star Ledger,* April 30, 1991.
10. Commerce & Industry Association of New Jersey, Legislative Bulletin, February 14, 1992.
11. Gordon Bishop, "State to Set Up Hot Line," *The Star Ledger,* February 25, 1990.
12. New Jersey Chamber of Commerce, "Executive Eye on Trenton, N.J.," (January 20, 1989), 4.
13. Judith A. Osborne, "Roundtable Discussion Trades Ideas," *The Star Ledger,* April 18, 1991.
14. Ibid.
15. Laurence T. Clark, Jr., "Eco Trends," *New Jersey Business Journal,* (March 1991), 26.

Chapter V

1. Commerce & Industry Association, "Survey Responses," Paramus, N.J., February 1991.
2. David Van Horn, "School Board Balks at $750,000 Pollution Fine," *The Star Ledger,* September 18, 1990.
3. Tom Johnson, "DEP Fines Firms," *The Star Ledger,* September 10, 1990.
4. Commerce & Industry Association, "Survey Responses," February 1991.
5. Porzio, Bromberg & Newman, "Environmental Update," Morristown, N.J., May 10, 1991.
6. Commerce & Industry Association, "Survey Responses," Paramus, N.J., February, 1991.

7. Fred J. Aun, "Montague Mayor Upset to Lose Land in Penalty," *Sunday Star Ledger,* September 15, 1991.

Chapter VI

1. Commerce & Industry Association, "Survey Responses."
2. Cyril Francus, "Letter to the Author," September 1989.
3. Commerce & Industry Association, "Survey Responses."
4. Warren T. Brookes, "The Global Warming Panic," *Forbes,* December 25, 1989, p. 102.
5. Lourdes Lee Valeriano, "Cleanup Rules are Called Threat to Credit Ratings," Wall Street Journal, June 26, 1991. Reprinted with permission of Dow Jones & Company, Inc. All rights reserved worldwide.
6. "Clean-up Costs are Called Threat to Industry Credit Worthiness," *Investors Daily,* May 20, 1991.
7. Keith Schneider,"Toxic Clean-Up Stalls Transfer of Military Sites," *The New York Times,* June 30, 1991.
8. Renee Rewiski, "Environmentalists Chasing Industry Out of New Jersey," *Northern New Jersey Business Journal,* November 27, 1989.
9. Bill Glovin, "Toxic Gold," *Rutgers Magazine,* Spring 1991, 7.
10. Ibid.
11. Tom Johnson, "Case Casts Double on DEP Power to Force Clean Up," *The Star Ledger,* September 13, 1990.
12. "Letter to the Editor," *The Star Ledger,* March 3, 1991.
13. Joseph Perone,"Hillside Plant to Close," *The Star Ledger,* October 18, 1989.

Chapter VII

1. Laura Michaelis, "Lenders Must Not Be Held Liable for Pollution Woes," *Investors Daily,* July 11, 1991.
2. Patrick J.O'Keefe, "Evidence Builds Up Against State Curbs," *Sunday Star Ledger,* March 3, 1991.

3. Stefan N. Gable, "Presentation to the Joint Appropriations Committee of the New Jersey Legislature," May 2, 1990.
4. Janet Moore, "ECRA Environmental Boon or Economic Bust," *Easton* (Pennsylvania), *Sunday Express,* January 6, 1991.
5. Ibid.
6. Clyde Folley, "Article," *New Jersey Business Journal,* (September 1991), 60.
7. Art Bianconi, "The Forum," *The Star Ledger,* May 6, 1991.
8. Porzio, Bromberg & Newman, "Environmental Update," August 30, 1991.

Chapter IX

1. Liv Osby, "26 Developers Find Plans on Shaky Ground," *The Morris County* (New Jersey) *Daily Record,* August 9, 1991.
2. Marcia Z. Taylor and Darrell Smith, "New Wetlands Rules Drain Farmers," *Farm Journal,* June 1990, 15.
3. Tom Johnson, "Jersey to Offer Bounties for Tips on Polluters," *The Star Ledger,* September 20, 1990.
4. Ibid.
5. Guy Sterling, "Environmental Prosecutor Seeks River Watchers," *The Star Ledger,* May 9, 1991.
6. Ibid.
7. Marcia Z. Taylor and Darrell Smith, "New Wetlands . . ."18, 19.
8. Paul Craig Roberts, "Economic Viewpoint," *Business Week* (June 10, 1991), 16. Reprinted with permission.
9. Ibid.
10. Warren T. Brookes, "The Global Warming Panic," *Forbes,* December 25, 1989, 96.
11. Rick Henderson, "Is California 40 Percent Wetlands," *New York Times,* April 3, 1991.

12. Peter Resota, "Letter to the Editor," *Daily Record,* July 10, 1991.
13. Fred J. Aun, "Mayor, Zoning Official Fighting DEP Actions," *The Star Ledger,* July 31, 1991.

Chapter X

1. Donald Warshaw, "Reports Underestimate Loss of Blue Collar Jobs," *The Star Ledger,* January 6, 1991.
2. Ibid.
3. Patricia Sullivan, "Personal Income Declines 0.2% in Jersey," *The Star Ledger,* July 24, 1991.
4. Donald Warshaw, "Jersey Loses Jobs for the 28th Month," *The Star Ledger,* July 31, 1991.
5. "ENR News, Hazardous Waste," *McGraw Hill Construction Weekly,* April 13, 1989, 8.
6. Ibid., 68.
7. Rick Butler, "Environmental Lawman Targets River Abuses," *The Star Ledger,* May 7, 1991.
8. Ibid.
9. Franklin T. Reick, "Bureaucracy at is Worst," Letter, Mahwah, N.J., May 12, 1991.
10. Richard T. Dewling, Letter to Assemblyman Garabed Haytaian, June 27, 1988.
11. Dixie Lee Ray and Lou Guzzo, "Trashing the Planet," Washington, D.C., *Regnery Gateway,* 1990, p. 171. Copyright, 1990 by Dixie Lee Ray and Lou Guzzo, all rights reserved. Reprinted by special permission from Regnery Gateway, Inc., Washington, D.C.
12. Illinois Environmental Protection Agency, Office of State Fire Marshall, Springfield, IL.
13. Jo Kwong, Ph.D., "Myths About Environmental Policy," Citizens for the Environment, Washington, D.C., 1991, p. 40.

14. Editorial, "The New Religion," reprinted with permission from the August 22, 1991, issue of the *New Jersey Law Journal*. Copyright 1991, *New Jersey Law Journal*.

Appendices

1. Summary of Decision, May 6, 1991, Appellate Division of Superior Court of New Jersey, re: ECRA Regulations.
2. "In the Clutches of the Superfund Mess," *The New York Times*, June 16, 1991. Reprinted with the permission of *The New York Times*.
3. Blank ECRA Forms, #001, #002, #009.
4. Warren County Economic Development Advisory Council, Recommendation, July 17, 1991.
5. ECRA Fee Structure as of April 2, 1992.